cook's library
Potatoes

cook's library
Potatoes

This is a Parragon Publishing Book
First published in 2003

Parragon Publishing
Queen Street House
4 Queen Street
Bath BA1 1HE, UK

ISBN: 0-75259-446-X

Printed in China

NOTE

This book uses imperial and metric measurements. Follow the same
units of measurement throughout; do not mix imperial and metric.
All spoon measurements are level: teaspoons are assumed to be 5 ml,
and tablespoons are assumed to be 15 ml. Unless otherwise stated,
milk is assumed to be whole, eggs and individual vegetables, such as
potatoes, are medium, and pepper is freshly ground black pepper.

The times given for each recipe are an approximate guide only because
the preparation times may differ according to the techniques used by
different people and the cooking times may vary as a result of the type
of oven used. The preparation times include chilling and marinating
times, where appropriate.

Recipes using raw or very lightly cooked eggs should be
avoided by infants, the elderly, pregnant women, convalescents,
and anyone suffering from an illness.

Contents

6   introduction

18   soups, salads, & appetizers

58   light meals & side dishes

108   vegetarian & vegan suppers

120   vegetable savories

138   fish dishes

148   poultry & meat

168   bread & cakes

174   index

Introduction

Easy to grow and cook, inexpensive, marvelously tasty, extremely nutritious, and highly versatile, the potato has unsurprisingly become one of the world's most popular vegetables and an important staple food, which is cultivated almost everywhere.

There is a vast range of different varieties of potato—around 3,000 in all—although only about 100 of these are regularly grown. Each variety has its own distinctive shape, texture, even color, and reflects its country of origin, from the firm yellow flesh of the Jersey Royal new potato to the rich, warm orange of the Caribbean yam.

Possibly dating as far back as 3000 BCE, the potato originated in South America, where it was known as the "papa." It was eaten by the Incas, fresh when it was in season and dried in winter. It was unknown to the rest of the world, however, until the 16th century, when Peru fell to the Spanish conquistador Francisco Pizarro. Peru was a country well known to be rich in minerals, and it was the mineral traders who began to introduce the potato elsewhere.

In Europe, the potato arrived via Spain, and its name gradually evolved from "papa" to "battata." It became famous not only for its nutritional value, but also for its healing properties. The Italians believed that the cooked flesh would heal a wound if rubbed into the infected area, and Pope Pius IV was sufficiently convinced of this to plant his own crop. From here, the potato moved northward through Switzerland, France, Germany, and Belgium, reaching the New World with the explorer

Francis Drake, who shared his cargo of potatoes with the starving English colonists. Sir Walter Raleigh later brought the potato to Britain. He also took it to Ireland, where the soil was perfect for growing it, and it became a dietary mainstay for the Irish peasantry, who survived for generations on little else.

Nutritionally, potatoes are an excellent source of starch for energy and fiber. They have a higher protein value than most plant foods, are very rich in vitamin C, and also contain vitamin B-complex, as well as minerals, especially potassium. However, many of the nutrients are found in or just below the skin, so it is essential to cook them in ways that will retain their health-promoting properties.

Although potatoes were once considered to be forbidden to slimmers, they are in fact a positive aid to weight control when cooked and served with the minimum of fat. Sufferers from stomach ulcers and arthritis will also benefit from drinking raw potato juice, although their taste buds may object to the flavor!

This book is a collection of some of the most delicious potato recipes, gathered from around the world. Whatever the occasion, these inspiring dishes will show you how this adaptable vegetable can be used in a multitude of ways to enhance your everyday eating.

Regional Cooking

Although the potato is known and grown throughout the world, the ways in which it is cooked and served vary enormously from country to country, and often depend on whether it is the main staple of a nation's diet.

The highest consumers are Russia, Poland, and Germany, followed by Holland, Cyprus, and Ireland. Elsewhere, the potato may be less popular than pasta, rice, or bread in the daily diet.

As Spain was the first European country to discover the potato, it is appropriate that it is used in one of the most popular and well-known classic Spanish dishes, tortilla. This is a substantial, crispy-coated vegetable omelet-like dish of eggs and thinly sliced waxy potatoes, to which may be added bell peppers, tomatoes, corn—the choice is unlimited. Variations of this omelet can be found all around the Mediterranean—a Greek version, for example, is to fill the potato omelet with a melting mixture of feta cheese and spinach.

In Italy, mealy potatoes are used in another classic dish—gnocchi. Here, the cooked potatoes are mashed until smooth, then mixed with flour, egg yolks, and olive oil to make little dumplings, which are cooked very quickly in boiling water and served with a sauce. Herbs or cheese may be added to the recipe, and a delicious variation is to add spinach. A similar base can also be used to make potato noodles.

From Ireland comes Colcannon—a marvelous mixture of mashed potatoes and shredded cabbage, topped with a pool of melted butter—which is usually served with a piece of bacon.

Worldwide, the potato is often used as a basis for a hearty salad. On the Mediterranean coast of France, for example, potatoes are combined with tuna and eggs as the base for the famous Salade Niçoise. In India, they may be mixed with broccoli and mango, and topped with a spicy yogurt dressing, while in Mexico sliced potatoes are topped with tomatoes, chiles, and ham and served with guacamole.

In Italy, potatoes are layered with sausage, radicchio, sun-dried tomatoes, and basil and drizzled with a tomato-flavored olive oil dressing, and in Russia the classic combination of cucumber and dill is often made more substantial by the addition of potatoes and beets.

The potato makes an excellent ingredient in soups, and in European cuisine, potatoes are used in a number of classic soup recipes—Vichyssoise, Pistou, and Bouillabaisse to name a few. Different cultures also have their own variations of chowder, a filling soup based on potatoes and milk. In New England, for example, fresh clams are added, while in Scotland the chowder is flavored with smoked haddock to make the intriguingly named Cullen Skink.

Even as an accompaniment, potatoes are served in a variety of ways. In India, they are mixed with other vegetables, readily absorbing all the spice flavors.

In France, layers of waxy potatoes are topped with heavy cream and sometimes cheese to make a rich and very filling classic dish, Potatoes Dauphinois. In Britain they are served roasted to a crisp with the traditional Sunday lunch, and in Belgium French fries are served with mayonnaise, for dipping.

Using Potatoes

The potato is without doubt one of the most versatile food items. However, not all types of potato are suitable for all purposes, and the following list gives the uses for some of the most popular varieties.

Russet Potatoes
The most popular variety in the US, this rough-skinned potato is excellent for baking, mashing, frying, and roasting.

Round White Potatoes
This medium-size variety is a good all-purpose type, which is ideal for boiling and mashing.

Round Red Potatoes
Available mostly in late summer and early fall, this variety has rosy red skin and white flesh. It is best used for salads, boiling, roasting, and steaming.

Fingerling Potatoes
The name given to small, thumb-size, baby Long White Potatoes.

New Potatoes
Any freshly dug young potatoes, which have not reached maturity. They are excellent when boiled or pan-roasted whole.

Blue and Purple Potatoes
Mostly available in the fall, this variety has a nutty flavor and bluish flesh. It is best suited for steaming and baking.

Sweet Potatoes and Yam
Sweet potatoes are best fried or boiled and sweeter yams are best roasted or mashed in cakes.

Buying and Storing

When choosing potatoes, make sure they are firm and well-shaped with a smooth, tight skin. New potatoes should be eaten as fresh as possible, but old potatoes can be stored in a cool, dark, dry place—exposure to light makes them turn green, resulting in an unpleasant flavor and a higher level of glycoalkaloids, which are naturally occurring toxins.

Preparation and Cooking

To preserve the nutritional value of potatoes, they should ideally be baked in their skins, or scrubbed rather than peeled. If peeled potatoes are required, they should be cooked in their skins and then peeled afterward.

Boiling

For new and old potatoes, put them in a pan, pour in enough boiling water to cover them, then add a lid to the pan and boil gently until tender.

Steaming

To steam new and old potatoes, put them into a steamer over a pan of boiling water, and then cook them gently until they are tender.

Mashing or Creaming

Boil the potatoes, then drain well. Add a piece of butter, season, then mash, preferably with an electric hand-whisk, or by hand, first with a potato masher and then stirring briskly with a fork. As a variation, add cream or mascarpone cheese as well as butter; use garlic-infused olive oil instead of butter; or add some fresh pesto sauce.

Roasting

Simmer the potatoes in boiling water for 10 minutes. Drain them, then shake them in the pan to roughen their surfaces. Tip them carefully into a roasting pan of very hot fat, and cook on the top shelf of a preheated oven, 425°F/220°C, for 45 minutes until golden and crispy.

Baking

Scrub, then dry the potatoes. Prick the skins, then rub them with olive oil and salt. Bake in a preheated oven, 425°F/220°C, for 1–1½ hours.

Deep-Frying

For deep-frying, the temperature of the oil is all-important and a deep-fat fryer would be a good investment. Parboiled, sliced, or diced potatoes can be sautéed in a little oil in a heavy-based pan.

How to Use This Book

Each recipe contains a wealth of useful information, including a breakdown of nutritional quantities, preparation and cooking times, and level of difficulty. All of this information is explained in detail below.

The ingredients for each recipe are listed in the order that they are used.

The nutritional information provided for each recipe is per serving or per portion. Optional ingredients, variations or serving suggestions have not been included in the calculations.

A full-color photograph of the finished dish.

The method is clearly explained with step-by-step instructions that are easy to follow.

Cook's Tips provide useful information regarding ingredients or cooking techniques.

⭐ The number of stars represents the difficulty of each recipe, ranging from very easy (1 star) to challenging (4 stars).

🕐 This amount of time represents the preparation of ingredients, including cooling, chilling, and soaking times.

🕐 This represents the cooking time.

Soups, Salads, *and* Appetizers

Potatoes form the basis of many delicious and easy-to-prepare home-made soups, because they are the perfect thickening agent while adding a subtle flavor. With the addition of just a few ingredients, you can have a selection of soups at your fingertips.

Also featured in this chapter are appetizers and salads based on potatoes. In addition to the creamy potato salads that are so popular, there are many other recipes to tempt your palate, including dishes suitable for light lunches as well as hearty entrées. Many of these recipes are also ideal choices for barbecues and picnics.

This simple recipe uses the sweet potato with its distinctive flavor and color, combined with a hint of orange and cilantro.

Sweet Potato *and* Onion Soup

SERVES 4

2 tbsp vegetable oil
generous 5 cups diced sweet potatoes
1 carrot, diced
2 onions, sliced
2 garlic cloves, crushed
2½ cups vegetable bouillon
1¼ cups unsweetened orange juice
1 cup plain lowfat unsweetened yogurt
2 tbsp chopped fresh cilantro
salt and pepper

to garnish
fresh cilantro sprigs
strips of orange rind

1 Heat the vegetable oil in a large pan and add the diced sweet potatoes and carrot, sliced onions, and garlic. Sauté the vegetables gently for 5 minutes, stirring constantly with a wooden spoon. Do not let color.

2 Pour in the vegetable bouillon and orange juice and bring them to a boil.

3 Reduce the heat to a simmer, then cover the pan and cook the vegetables for 20 minutes or until the sweet potato and carrot cubes are tender.

4 Transfer the mixture to a food processor or blender, in batches, and process or blend for 1 minute until puréed. Return the purée to the rinsed-out pan.

5 Stir in the unsweetened yogurt and chopped cilantro and season to taste with salt and pepper.

6 Ladle the soup into 4 warmed bowls and garnish with a few sprigs of fresh cilantro and orange rind. Serve.

NUTRITION
Calories *320*; Sugars *26 g*; Protein *7 g*;
Carbohydrate *62 g*; Fat *7 g*; Saturates *1 g*

easy

15 mins

30 mins

From pantry ingredients, this spicy and substantial soup makes a delicious meal-in-a-bowl, ideal for a midweek supper.

Potato *and* Garbanzo Bean Soup

1 Heat the olive oil in a large pan over medium heat. Add the onion and garlic and cook for 3–4 minutes, stirring occasionally, until the onion is beginning to soften. Do not let color.

2 Add the carrot, potatoes, turmeric, garam masala, and curry powder to the onion and garlic and continue cooking for 1–2 minutes.

3 Add the tomatoes, water, and chili paste with a large pinch of salt. Reduce the heat, then cover and let simmer for 30 minutes, stirring occasionally.

4 Add the garbanzo beans and peas to the pan and cook for about 15 minutes or until all the vegetables are tender.

5 Taste the soup and adjust the seasoning, if needed, adding a little more chili, if wished. Ladle into 4 warmed soup bowls and sprinkle with cilantro.

SERVES 4

1 tbsp olive oil
1 large onion, chopped finely
2–3 garlic cloves, chopped finely or crushed
1 carrot, cut into fourths and thinly sliced
2 cups diced potatoes
¼ tsp ground turmeric
¼ tsp garam masala
¼ tsp mild curry powder
14 oz/400 g canned chopped tomatoes in juice
3¾ cups water
¼ tsp chili paste, or to taste
14 oz/400 g canned garbanzo beans, rinsed and drained
3 oz/85 g fresh or frozen peas
salt and pepper
chopped fresh cilantro, to garnish

NUTRITION
Calories *40*; Sugars *1.6 g*; Protein *1.8 g*; Carbohydrate *6.5 g*; Fat *1 g*; Saturates *0.1 g*

⊛⊛⊛ moderate

◔ 5 mins

◕ 50 mins

⊛ **COOK'S TIP**

If preferred, purée the soup in a blender.

A slightly hot and spicy Indian flavor is given to this soup with the use of garam masala, chile, cumin, and cilantro.

Indian Potato *and* Pea Soup

SERVES 4

2 tbsp vegetable oil
1¼ cups diced mealy potatoes
1 large onion, chopped
2 garlic cloves, crushed
1 tsp garam masala
1 tsp ground coriander
1 tsp ground cumin
3¾ cups vegetable bouillon
1 fresh red chile, chopped
3½ oz/100 g frozen peas
4 tbsp plain unsweetened yogurt
salt and pepper
chopped fresh cilantro, to garnish

1 Heat the vegetable oil in a large pan over low heat. Add the diced potatoes, onion, and garlic and sauté gently for about 5 minutes, stirring constantly.

2 Add the ground spices and cook for 1 minute, stirring all the time.

3 Stir in the vegetable bouillon and chopped red chile and bring the mixture to a boil. Reduce the heat, then cover the pan and let simmer for 20 minutes, until the potatoes begin to break down.

4 Add the peas and cook for another 5 minutes. Stir in the yogurt and season to taste with salt and pepper.

5 Ladle into 4 warmed soup bowls. Garnish the soup with chopped fresh cilantro and serve hot.

NUTRITION
Calories *160*; Sugars *8 g*; Protein *6 g*; Carbohydrate *21 g*; Fat *7 g*; Saturates *1 g*

⭐ very easy

🕐 5 mins

🕐 35 mins

👨‍🍳 COOK'S TIP

For slightly less heat, seed the chile before adding it to the soup. Always wash your hands after handling chiles because they contain volatile oils that can irritate the skin and make your eyes burn if you touch your face.

This creamy soup has a delightful pale green coloring and rich flavor from the blend of tender broccoli and blue cheese.

Broccoli *and* Potato Soup

1 Heat the olive oil in a large pan over low heat. Add the diced potatoes and onion and sauté the vegetables gently for 5 minutes, stirring constantly.

2 Set aside a few broccoli florets for the garnish and add the remaining broccoli to the pan. Add the cheese and bouillon.

3 Bring to a boil, then reduce the heat, cover the pan, and let simmer for 25 minutes until the potatoes are tender.

4 Transfer the soup to a food processor or blender in 2 batches and process until the mixture is a smooth purée.

5 Return the purée to a clean pan and stir in the cream and a pinch of paprika. Season to taste with salt and pepper.

6 Blanch the reserved broccoli florets in a pan of boiling water for about 2 minutes, then drain with a draining spoon.

7 Ladle the soup into 4 warmed bowls and garnish with the broccoli florets and a sprinkling of paprika. Serve at once.

SERVES 4

2 tbsp olive oil
$2^2/_3$ cups diced potatoes
1 onion, diced
8 oz/225 g broccoli florets
$4^1/_2$ oz/125 g blue cheese, crumbled
$4^1/_2$ cups vegetable bouillon
$^2/_3$ cup heavy cream
pinch of paprika, plus extra to garnish
salt and pepper

NUTRITION
Calories *452*; Sugars *4 g*; Protein *14 g*;
Carbohydrate *20 g*; Fat *35 g*; Saturates *19 g*

⭐ very easy
🕐 5–10 mins
🕐 35 mins

👨‍🍳 COOK'S TIP

This soup freezes very successfully. Follow the method described here up to Step 4, and freeze the soup after it has been puréed. Add the cream and paprika just before serving. Garnish and serve.

The many varieties of dried mushrooms available are relatively expensive, but the concentrated flavor that they add to a dish justifies the cost.

Potato *and* Mushroom Soup

SERVES 4

2 tbsp vegetable oil
1 lb 5 oz/600 g mealy potatoes, sliced
1 onion, sliced
2 garlic cloves, crushed
4½ cups beef bouillon
1 oz/25 g dried mushrooms
2 celery stalks, sliced
2 tbsp brandy
salt and pepper

topping

3 tbsp butter
2 thick slices white bread, crusts removed
3 tbsp freshly grated Parmesan cheese

to garnish

rehydrated dried mushrooms
fresh parsley sprigs

1 Heat the vegetable oil in a large skillet over low heat. Add the potato, onion slices, and garlic and sauté for 5 minutes, stirring constantly.

2 Add the beef bouillon, dried mushrooms, and sliced celery. Bring to a boil, then reduce the heat to a simmer, cover the pan, and cook the soup for 20 minutes until the potatoes are tender.

3 Meanwhile, melt the butter for the topping in the skillet. Sprinkle the bread slices with the grated Parmesan cheese and cook the slices in the butter for 1 minute on each side until crisp. Cut each slice into triangles.

4 Stir the brandy into the soup. Season to taste with salt and pepper, then pour into warmed bowls and top with the triangles. Garnish with a few mushrooms and sprigs of fresh parsley and serve.

NUTRITION
Calories *81*; Sugars *0.7 g*; Protein *3.8 g*;
Carbohydrate *7.6 g*; Fat *4 g*; Saturates *1.8 g*

moderate

5 mins

30 mins

🍄 **COOK'S TIP**

Probably the most popular dried mushroom is the cep, but any variety will add a lovely flavor to this soup. If you do not wish to use dried mushrooms, add 4½ oz/125 g sliced fresh mushrooms of your choice to the soup.

This is a really filling soup, which should be served before a light main course. It is easy to prepare and filled with flavor.

Vegetable *and* Corn Chowder

1 Heat the vegetable oil in a large pan over low heat. Add the onion, bell pepper, garlic, and potato and sauté, stirring frequently, for 2–3 minutes.

2 Stir in the flour and cook, stirring for 30 seconds. Gradually stir in the milk and vegetable bouillon.

3 Add the broccoli and corn. Bring the mixture to a boil, stirring constantly, then reduce the heat and let simmer for about 20 minutes or until all the vegetables are tender.

4 Add ½ cup of the cheese and stir until it melts.

5 Season to taste with salt and pepper, then spoon the chowder into a warmed soup tureen. Garnish with the remaining cheese and chopped cilantro and serve.

SERVES 4

1 tbsp vegetable oil
1 red onion, diced
1 red bell pepper, seeded and diced
3 garlic cloves, crushed
1¾ cups diced potatoes
2 tbsp all-purpose flour
2½ cups milk
1¼ cups vegetable bouillon
1¾ oz/50 g broccoli florets
3 cups canned corn, drained
¾ cup freshly grated Colby cheese
salt and pepper
1 tbsp chopped fresh cilantro, to garnish

NUTRITION
Calories *378*; Sugars *20 g*; Protein *16 g*;
Carbohydrate *52 g*; Fat *13 g*; Saturates *6 g*

very easy
15 mins
30 mins

COOK'S TIP

Vegetarian cheeses are made with rennets of nonanimal origin.

It is hard to imagine that celery root, a coarse, knobbly vegetable, can taste so sweet. It makes a marvelously flavorful soup.

Celery Root *and* Leek Soup

SERVES 4

1 tbsp butter
1 onion, chopped
2 large leeks, halved lengthwise and sliced
1 large celery root, peeled and cubed
8 oz/225 g potatoes, cubed
1 carrot, cut into fourths and thinly sliced
5 cups water
1/8 tsp dried marjoram
1 bay leaf
freshly grated nutmeg
salt and pepper
celery leaves, to garnish

1 Melt the butter in a large pan over medium–low heat. Add the onion and leeks and cook for about 4 minutes, stirring frequently, until just softened. Do not let color.

2 Add the celery root, potato, carrot, water, marjoram, and bay leaf, with a large pinch of salt. Bring to a boil, then reduce the heat, cover, and let simmer for about 25 minutes until the vegetables are tender. Remove the bay leaf.

3 Let the soup cool slightly. Transfer to a blender or food processor and purée until smooth. (If using a food processor, strain off the cooking liquid and set aside. Purée the soup solids with enough cooking liquid to moisten them, then combine with the remaining liquid.)

4 Return the puréed soup to the pan and stir to blend. Season with salt, pepper, and nutmeg. Let simmer over medium–low heat until reheated.

5 Ladle the soup into 4 warmed bowls, garnish with celery leaves and serve.

NUTRITION
Calories *20*; Sugars *1.3 g*; Protein *1.3 g*;
Carbohydrate *2.7 g*; Fat *0.7 g*; Saturates *0.4 g*

moderate

10 mins

35 mins

Fresh fava beans are best for this delicious soup, but if they are unavailable, use frozen beans instead.

Fava Bean *and* Mint Soup

1 Heat the olive oil in a large pan over low heat. Add the onion and garlic and sauté for 2–3 minutes until softened.

2 Add the potatoes and cook, stirring constantly, for 5 minutes.

3 Stir in the beans and the vegetable bouillon. Cover and let simmer for about 30 minutes or until the beans and potatoes are tender.

4 Remove a few vegetables with a draining spoon and set aside. Place the remainder of the soup in a food processor or blender and process until the soup is very smooth.

5 Return the soup to a clean pan and add the reserved vegetables and chopped mint. Stir thoroughly and heat through gently.

6 Transfer the soup to a warmed tureen or individual serving bowls. Garnish with swirls of yogurt and a few sprigs of fresh mint and serve at once.

SERVES 4

2 tbsp olive oil
1 red onion, chopped
2 garlic cloves, crushed
2²/₃ cups diced potatoes
3 cups fava beans, thawed if frozen
3³/₄ cups vegetable bouillon
2 tbsp chopped fresh mint

to garnish
fresh mint sprigs
plain unsweetened yogurt

NUTRITION
Calories *224*; Sugars *4 g*; Protein *12 g*; Carbohydrate *31 g*; Fat *6 g*; Saturates *1 g*

⭐ very easy

🕐 15 mins

🕐 40 mins

🍳 **COOK'S TIP**

Use chopped fresh cilantro and ½ teaspoon ground cumin as flavorings in the fava bean soup, if you prefer.

The combination of potato, garlic, and onion works marvelously in soup. In this recipe the garlic is roasted to give it added dimension and depth.

Roasted Garlic *and* Potato Soup

SERVES 4

1 large bulb of garlic with large cloves, peeled (about 3½ oz/100 g)
2 tsp olive oil
2 large leeks, sliced thinly
1 large onion, chopped finely
2¾ cups diced potatoes
5 cups chicken or vegetable bouillon
1 bay leaf
⅔ cup light cream
freshly grated nutmeg
lemon juice, optional
salt and pepper
chopped fresh chives, to garnish
crusty bread or toast, to serve

NUTRITION
Calories *240*; Sugars *7 g*; Protein *8 g*;
Carbohydrate *33 g*; Fat *10 g*; Saturates *5 g*

✪✪✪   moderate
🕐   10 mins
🕐   1 hr

1 Put the garlic cloves into a baking dish. Lightly brush with a little olive oil and bake in a preheated oven, 350°F/180°C, for 20 minutes until golden.

2 Heat the olive oil in a large pan over medium heat. Add the leeks and onion, then cover and cook for about 3 minutes, stirring frequently, until the vegetables begin to soften.

3 Add the potatoes, roasted garlic, bouillon, and bay leaf. Season to taste with salt (unless the bouillon is salty) and pepper. Bring to a boil, then reduce the heat, cover, and cook gently for about 30 minutes or until the vegetables are tender. Remove and discard the bay leaf.

4 Let the soup cool slightly, then transfer to a blender or food processor and purée until smooth, working in batches, if necessary. (If using a food processor, strain off the cooking liquid and set aside. Purée the soup solids with enough cooking liquid to moisten them, then combine with the remaining liquid.)

5 Return the soup to the pan and stir in the cream and a generous grating of nutmeg. Taste and adjust the seasoning, if necessary, adding a few drops of lemon juice, if wished. Reheat over low heat. Ladle into warmed soup bowls, then garnish with chives and serve with crusty bread or toast.

The addition of watercress, or arugula, to a traditional vichyssoise gives it a refreshing flavor and lovely cool color.

Watercress Vichyssoise

1 Heat the olive oil in a heavy-based pan over medium heat. Add the leeks and cook for about 3 minutes, stirring frequently, until they begin to soften.

2 Add the potato, bouillon, water, and bay leaf. Add salt if the bouillon is unsalted. Bring to a boil, then reduce the heat, cover, and cook gently for about 25 minutes until the vegetables are tender. Remove and discard the bay leaf.

3 Add the watercress and continue to cook for another 2–3 minutes, stirring frequently, until the watercress is completely wilted.

4 Let the soup cool slightly, then transfer to a blender or food processor and purée until smooth, working in batches, if necessary. (If using a food processor, strain off the cooking liquid and set aside. Purée the soup solids with enough cooking liquid to moisten them, then combine with the remaining liquid.)

5 Put the soup into a large bowl and stir in half the cream. Season with salt, if needed, and plenty of pepper. Let cool to room temperature.

6 Let chill in the refrigerator until cold. Taste and adjust the seasoning, if needed. Ladle the watercress vichyssoise into chilled bowls, then drizzle the remaining cream on top and garnish with watercress leaves, to serve.

SERVES 6

1 tbsp olive oil
3 large leeks, sliced thinly
2 cups finely diced potatoes
2½ cups chicken or vegetable bouillon
2 cups water
1 bay leaf
6 oz/175 g prepared watercress, or arugula
¾ cup light cream
salt and pepper
watercress leaves, to garnish

NUTRITION
Calories 42; Sugars 0.8 g; Protein 2.1 g; Carbohydrate 3.6 g; Fat 2.2 g; Saturates 1 g

⭐   very easy

🕐   15 mins

🕐   35 mins

This soup makes a marvelous late-fall or winter appetizer. It has a delicious texture and cheerful golden color.

Sweet Potato *and* Apple Soup

SERVES 6

1 tbsp butter
3 leeks, sliced thinly
1 large carrot, sliced thinly
1 lb 5 oz/600 g sweet potatoes, peeled and cubed
2 large tart eating apples, peeled and cubed
5 cups water
freshly grated nutmeg
1 cup apple juice
1 cup whipping or light cream
salt and pepper

to garnish
chopped fresh chives
bunches of fresh chives

1 Melt the butter in a large pan over medium–low heat. Add the leeks, then cover and cook for 6–8 minutes or until softened, stirring frequently.

2 Add the carrot, sweet potatoes, apples, and water. Season with salt, pepper, and nutmeg. Bring to a boil, then reduce the heat and let simmer, covered, for about 20 minutes, stirring occasionally, until the vegetables are tender.

3 Let the soup cool slightly, then transfer to a blender or food processor and purée until smooth, working in batches, if necessary. (If using a food processor, strain off the cooking liquid and set aside. Purée the soup solids with enough cooking liquid to moisten them, then combine with the remaining liquid.)

4 Return the puréed soup to the pan and stir in the apple juice. Place over low heat and let simmer for about 10 minutes until heated through.

5 Stir in the cream and continue simmering for about 5 minutes, stirring frequently, until heated through. Taste and adjust the seasoning, adding more salt, pepper, and nutmeg, if necessary. Ladle the soup into warmed bowls, garnish with chopped chives and bunches of fresh chives, and serve.

NUTRITION
Calories 57; Sugars 3.8 g; Protein 0.7 g;
Carbohydrate 7.4 g; Fat 2.9 g; Saturates 1.8 g

⭐⭐⭐   moderate
🕐   10 mins
🕐   45 mins

This is a classic creamy soup made from potatoes and leeks. To achieve the delicate pale color, be sure to use only the white parts of the leeks.

Vichyssoise

1 Trim the leeks and remove the green part. Using a sharp knife slice the white part of the leeks very finely.

2 Melt the butter or margarine in a pan over low heat. Add the leeks and onion and bouillon, stirring occasionally, for 5 minutes without browning.

3 Add the potatoes, vegetable bouillon, lemon juice, nutmeg, coriander, and bay leaf to the pan. Season to taste with salt and pepper and bring to a boil. Cover and let simmer for about 30 minutes until all the vegetables are soft.

4 Let the soup cool slightly. Remove and discard the bay leaf and then press through a strainer or process in a food processor or blender until smooth. Pour the soup into a clean pan.

5 Blend the egg yolk into the cream. Add a little of the soup to the egg mixture and then whisk it all back into the soup. Reheat gently, without boiling. Taste and adjust the seasoning, if needed. Let cool and then let chill in the refrigerator.

6 Ladle the chilled soup into large soup bowls, garnish with chopped chives and a handful of fresh chives, then serve.

SERVES 4

3 large leeks
3 tbsp butter or margarine
1 onion, sliced thinly
1 lb 2 oz/500 g potatoes, chopped
3½ cups vegetable bouillon
2 tsp lemon juice
pinch of ground nutmeg
¼ tsp ground coriander
1 bay leaf
1 egg yolk
⅔ cup light cream
salt and white pepper

to garnish
chopped fresh chives
handfuls of fresh chives

NUTRITION
Calories *208*; Sugars *5 g*; Protein *5 g*;
Carbohydrate *20 g*; Fat *12 g*; Saturates *6 g*

⭐ very easy

🕐 10 mins

🕐 40 mins

This chunky aromatic soup is perfect for a cold-weather lunch or supper served with crusty bread and a salad, if wished.

Smoked Haddock Soup

SERVES 4

1 tbsp oil
⅓ cup bacon, cut into thin sticks
1 large onion, chopped finely
2 tbsp all-purpose flour
4 cups milk
1 lb 9 oz/700 g potatoes, cubed
6 oz/175 g skinless smoked haddock
salt and pepper
finely chopped fresh parsley, to garnish

1 Heat the oil in a large pan over medium heat. Add the bacon and cook for 2 minutes. Stir in the onion and continue cooking for 5–7 minutes, stirring frequently, until the onion is soft and the bacon golden. Tip the pan and spoon off as much fat as possible.

2 Stir in the flour and continue cooking for 2 minutes. Add half of the milk and stir well, scraping the bottom of the pan to mix in the flour.

3 Add the potatoes and remaining milk and season with pepper. Bring just to a boil, stirring frequently, then reduce the heat and let simmer, partially covered, for 10 minutes.

4 Add the smoked haddock and continue cooking, stirring occasionally, for 15 minutes or until the potatoes are tender and the fish breaks up easily.

5 Taste the soup and adjust the seasoning (salt may not be needed). Ladle into a warmed tureen or 4 large soup bowls and sprinkle with chopped parsley.

NUTRITION
Calories *80*; Sugars *2.9 g*; Protein *4.3 g*;
Carbohydrate *9.6 g*; Fat *3 g*; Saturates *1.4 g*

easy

5–10 mins

40 mins

🍳 **COOK'S TIP**

Cutting the potatoes into small cubes not only looks attractive, but lets them cook more quickly and evenly.

Fishermen's soups vary, depending on the season and the catch. Monkfish has a texture a little like lobster, but cod is equally appealing.

Breton Fish Soup *with* Cider

1 Melt the butter in a large pan over medium–low heat. Add the leek and shallots and cook for about 5 minutes, stirring frequently, until they begin to soften. Add the cider and bring to a boil.

2 Stir in the bouillon, potatoes, and bay leaf with a large pinch of salt (unless the bouillon is salty) and bring back to a boil. Reduce the heat, then cover and cook gently for 10 minutes.

3 Put the flour into a small bowl and very slowly whisk in a few tablespoons of the milk to make a thick paste. Stir in a little more to make a smooth liquid.

4 Adjust the heat so the soup bubbles gently. Stir in the flour mixture and cook, stirring frequently, for 5 minutes. Add the remaining milk and half the cream. Continue cooking for about 10 minutes until the potatoes are tender.

5 Combine the sorrel with the remaining cream. (If using a food processor, add the sorrel and chop, then add the cream and process briefly.)

6 Stir the sorrel cream into the soup and add the fish. Continue cooking, stirring occasionally, for about 3 minutes until the monkfish stiffens or the cod just begins to flake. Taste the soup and adjust the seasoning, if needed. Ladle the soup into 4 warmed soup bowls and serve.

SERVES 4

2 tsp butter
1 large leek, sliced thinly
2 shallots, chopped finely
½ cup hard cider
1¼ cups fish bouillon
9 oz/250 g potatoes, diced
1 bay leaf
4 tbsp all-purpose flour
¾ cup milk
¾ cup heavy cream
2 oz/55 g fresh sorrel leaves chopped finely
12 oz/350 g skinless monkfish or cod fillet, cut into 1-inch/2.5-cm pieces
salt and pepper

NUTRITION
Calories *103*; Sugars *1.5 g*; Protein *5.2 g*; Carbohydrate *6.6 g*; Fat *6.3 g*; Saturates *3.8 g*

⭐⭐   easy

🕐   5–10 mins

🕐   40 mins

This light and refreshing soup is also good served cold. An ideal appetizer for a summer meal, served with crunchy Melba toast.

Fennel *and* Tomato Soup

SERVES 4

2 tsp olive oil
1 large onion, halved and sliced
2 large fennel bulbs, halved and sliced
1 small potato, diced
3¾ cups water
1²/₃ cups tomato juice
1 bay leaf
4½ oz/125 g cooked small shrimp, shelled
2 tomatoes, peeled, seeded, and chopped
½ tsp chopped fresh dill
salt and pepper
fresh dill sprigs or fennel fronds, to garnish

1 Heat the olive oil in a large pan over medium heat. Add the onion and fennel and cook for 3–4 minutes, stirring occasionally.

2 Add the potato, water, tomato juice, and bay leaf with a large pinch of salt. Reduce the heat, then cover and let simmer for about 25 minutes, stirring once or twice, until the vegetables are soft.

3 Let cool slightly, then transfer to a blender or food processor. Purée until smooth, working in batches, if necessary. (If using a food processor, strain off the cooking liquid and set aside. Purée the soup solids with enough cooking liquid to moisten them, then mix with the remaining liquid.)

4 Return the soup to the pan and add the shrimp. Let simmer gently for about 10 minutes to reheat the soup and let it absorb the shrimp flavor.

5 Stir in the tomatoes and dill. Taste and adjust the seasoning, adding salt, if needed, and pepper. Thin the soup with a little more tomato juice, if wished. Ladle into 4 warmed soup bowls, garnish with dill sprigs or fennel fronds and serve.

NUTRITION
Calories *110*; Sugars *8 g*; Protein *10 g*;
Carbohydrate *13 g*; Fat *2 g*; Saturates *0 g*

⭐ very easy

🕐 30 mins

🕐 40 mins

This is a traditional, creamy Scottish soup. Some fresh cod has been added to balance the strong flavor of the smoked haddock.

Cullen Skink

1 Put the haddock fillet into a large skillet and cover with boiling water. Let stand for 10 minutes. Drain, reserving 1¼ cups of the soaking water. Flake the fish, taking care to remove all the bones.

2 Heat the butter in a large pan over low heat. Add the onion and cook gently for 10 minutes until softened. Add the milk and bring to a gentle simmer before adding the potato. Cook for 10 minutes.

3 Add the reserved haddock flakes and cod. Let simmer for another 10 minutes until the cod is tender.

4 Remove about one-third of the fish and potatoes, then put it in a food processor and process until smooth. Alternatively, press through a strainer into a bowl. Return to the soup with the cream, parsley, and seasoning. Taste and add a little lemon juice, if wished. Add a little of the reserved soaking water if the soup seems too thick. Reheat gently. Ladle the soup into 4 large, warmed bowls, garnish with lemon slices and a few sprigs of fresh parsley and serve at once.

SERVES 4

8 oz/225 g undyed smoked haddock fillet
2 tbsp butter
1 onion, chopped finely
2½ cups milk
2 cups diced potatoes
12 oz/350 g cod, boned, skinned, and cubed
⅔ cup heavy cream
2 tbsp chopped fresh parsley
lemon juice, to taste
salt and pepper

to garnish
lemon slices
fresh parsley sprigs

NUTRITION
Calories *108*; Sugars *2.3 g*; Protein *7.4 g*; Carbohydrate *5.6 g*; Fat *6.4 g*; Saturates *3.9 g*

⭐⭐⭐   moderate

🕐   20 mins

🕐   40 mins

🍳 **COOK'S TIP**

Look for Finnan haddock, if you can find it. If unavailable, use undyed haddock, but try not to use yellow dyed haddock fillet.

This hearty soup of beans and vegetables is from Nice, and gets its name from the fresh basil sauce, which is stirred in at the last minute.

Pistou

SERVES 4

2 young carrots
1 lb/450 g potatoes
7 oz/200 g fresh peas in the shells
7 oz/200 g thin green beans
5½ oz/150 g young zucchini
2 tbsp olive oil
1 garlic clove, crushed
1 large onion, chopped finely
10 cups vegetable bouillon or water
1 bouquet garni of 2 sprigs of fresh parsley
    and 1 bay leaf tied in a 3-inch/7.5-cm piece
    of celery
3 oz/85 g dried small soup pasta
1 large tomato, peeled, seeded, and chopped
    or diced
fresh Parmesan cheese shavings, to serve

pistou sauce
1½ cups fresh basil leaves
1 garlic clove
5 tbsp fruity extra virgin olive oil
salt and pepper

NUTRITION

Calories 55; Sugars 1.2 g; Protein 3.8 g;
Carbohydrate 4.2 g; Fat 2.6 g; Saturates 0.6 g

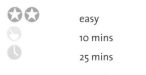
easy
10 mins
25 mins

1 To make the pistou sauce, put the basil leaves, garlic, and olive oil into a food processor and process until well blended. Season to taste with salt and pepper. Transfer to a bowl, then cover and let chill until required.

2 Peel the carrots and cut them in half lengthwise, then slice. Peel the potatoes and cut into quarter lengths, then slice. Let stand in a bowl of water until required, to prevent discoloration.

3 Shell the peas. Top and tail the green beans and cut them into 1-inch/2.5-cm pieces. Cut the zucchini in half lengthwise, then slice.

4 Heat the olive oil in a large pan or flameproof casserole over low heat. Add the garlic and cook for 2 minutes, stirring. Add the onion and cook for 2 minutes until softened. Add the carrots and potatoes and stir for 30 seconds.

5 Pour in the bouillon and bring to a boil. Reduce the heat, then partially cover and let simmer for 8 minutes until the vegetables begin to become tender.

6 Stir in the peas, beans, zucchini, bouquet garni, pasta, and tomato. Season to taste and cook for 4 minutes or until the vegetables and pasta are tender. Stir in the pistou sauce and serve with shavings of Parmesan cheese.

This mildly spiced, rich green soup is delicately scented with ginger and lemon grass. It makes a good light appetizer or summer lunch dish.

Spinach *and* Ginger Soup

1 Heat the corn oil in a large pan over low heat. Add the onion, garlic, and ginger, and cook gently for 3–4 minutes until softened, but not browned.

2 Set aside 2–3 small spinach leaves. Add the remaining leaves and lemongrass to the pan, stirring until the spinach is wilted. Add the bouillon and potato to the pan and bring to a boil. Reduce the heat, cover, and let simmer for about 10 minutes.

3 Tip the soup into a food processor or blender and process until smooth.

4 Return the soup to the pan and add the Chinese rice wine, then adjust the seasoning to taste with salt and pepper. Heat until just about to boil.

5 Finely shred the 2–3 reserved spinach leaves and sprinkle some over the top. Drizzle with a few drops of sesame oil and serve hot, garnished with more finely shredded fresh spinach leaves.

SERVES 4

2 tbsp corn oil
1 onion, chopped
2 garlic cloves, chopped finely
2 tsp fresh gingerroot, chopped finely
4 cups fresh young spinach leaves
1 small lemongrass stem, chopped finely
4 cups chicken or vegetable bouillon
8 oz/225 g potato, peeled and chopped
1 tbsp Chinese rice wine or dry sherry
1 tsp sesame oil
salt and pepper
fresh spinach, shredded finely, to garnish

NUTRITION
Calories *38*; Sugars *0.8 g*; Protein *3.2 g*;
Carbohydrate *2.4 g*; Fat *1.8 g*; Saturates *0.2 g*

⭐⭐ easy

🕐 5–10 mins

🕐 25 mins

COOK'S TIP

To make a creamy spinach and coconut soup, stir in 4 tablespoons creamed coconut, or replace 1¼ cups of the bouillon with coconut milk.

This soup makes a festive seafood extravaganza worthy of any special occasion or celebration.

Bouillabaisse

SERVES 6

1 lb/450 g jumbo shrimp
1 lb 10 oz/750 g firm white fish fillets, such as sea bass, snapper, and monkfish
4 tbsp olive oil
grated rind of 1 orange
1 large garlic clove, chopped finely
½ tsp chili paste or harissa
1 large leek, sliced
1 onion, halved and sliced
1 red bell pepper, seeded and sliced
3–4 tomatoes, cored and cut into 8 pieces
4 garlic cloves, sliced
1 bay leaf
pinch of saffron threads
½ tsp fennel seeds
2½ cups water
5 cups fish bouillon
1 fennel bulb, chopped finely
1 large onion, chopped finely
8 oz/225 g potatoes, halved and thinly sliced
9 oz/250 g scallops
salt and pepper
toasted French bread slices and store-bought aïoli, to serve

NUTRITION

Calories 55; Sugars 1.1 g; Protein 7.2 g; Carbohydrate 2.6 g; Fat 1.8 g; Saturates 0.3 g

★★★ moderate

🕐 10 mins

🕐 1 hr 5 mins

1 Shell the shrimp and set aside the shells. Cut the fish into pieces 2 inches/ 5 cm square. Trim any ragged edges and set aside. Put the fish into a bowl with 2 tablespoons of the olive oil, the orange rind, crushed garlic, and chili paste. Turn to coat, cover, and let chill in the refrigerator. Let the shrimp and fish chill separately.

2 Heat 1 tablespoon of the olive oil in a large pan over medium heat. Add the leek, onion, and bell pepper. Cover and cook for 5 minutes, stirring, until the onion softens. Stir in the tomatoes, garlic, bay leaf, saffron, fennel seeds, shrimp shells, water, and fish bouillon. Bring the bouillon to a boil, reduce the heat, and let simmer, covered, for 30 minutes. Strain and set aside.

3 Heat the remaining olive oil in a large pan. Add the fennel and onion and cook for 4–5 minutes until the onion softens, stirring frequently. Add the reserved bouillon and potatoes and bring to a boil. Reduce the heat slightly, cover, and cook for 12–15 minutes or until the potatoes are just tender.

4 Reduce the heat to a simmer and add the fish, beginning with any thicker pieces and putting in the thinner ones after 2–3 minutes. Add the shrimp and scallops and let simmer until all the seafood is cooked and opaque.

5 Taste the soup and adjust the seasoning, if needed. Ladle into 6 large, warmed soup bowls. Spread the aïoli on the toasted bread slices and arrange on top of the soup.

This soup can be made in stages, so it is ideal for entertaining because some of it can be prepared in advance.

Mussel *and* Potato Soup

1 Discard any broken mussels and those with open shells that do not close when tapped. Wash under cold running water, pull off any "beards," and scrape off barnacles with a knife. Put the mussels into a large, heavy-based pan. Cover tightly and cook over high heat for about 4 minutes or until the mussels open.

2 When cool enough to handle, remove the mussels from the shells, adding any additional juices to the cooking liquid. Strain the cooking liquid into a bowl through a cheesecloth-lined strainer and set aside.

3 Put the flour in a mixing bowl and very slowly whisk in a few tablespoons of the milk to form a thick paste. Stir in a little more to make a smooth liquid.

4 Put the remaining milk, cream, and garlic into a pan and bring to a boil. Whisk in the flour mixture. Reduce the heat to medium–low and let simmer for about 15 minutes until the garlic is tender and the liquid has thickened slightly. Drop in the parsley leaves and cook for 2–3 minutes.

5 Let the soup base cool slightly, then process in a blender until smooth.

6 Return the soup to the pan and stir in the potatoes. Season to taste with salt and pepper and let simmer gently for 5–7 minutes. Add the mussels and cook for about 2 minutes until the soup is steaming. Ladle into 4 warmed bowls, garnish with lemon slices, a few sprigs of fresh dill, and serve.

SERVES 4

2 lb 4 oz/1 kg mussels
3 tbsp all-purpose flour
2½ cups milk
1¼ cups whipping cream
1–2 garlic cloves, chopped finely
6 cups curly parsley leaves (1 large bunch)
10½ oz/300 g cooked potatoes, diced
salt and pepper

to garnish
lemon slices
fresh dill sprigs

NUTRITION
Calories *95*; Sugars *1.8 g*; Protein *3.7 g*; Carbohydrate *6.4 g*; Fat *6.2 g*; Saturates *3.7 g*

easy

15 mins

45 mins

This meal-in-a-soup is originally from the beautiful area of Moira, in Northern Ireland.

Tom's Chicken Soup

SERVES 4

3 smoked bacon slices, chopped
1 lb 2 oz/500 g skinless, boneless
   chicken, chopped
2 tbsp butter
1 lb 8 oz/675 g potatoes, chopped
3 onions, chopped
2½ cups giblet or chicken bouillon
2½ cups milk
⅔ cup heavy cream
2 tbsp chopped fresh parsley
salt and pepper
soda bread, to serve

1 Gently cook the chopped bacon and chicken in a large pan over low heat for 10 minutes.

2 Add the butter, potatoes, and onions and cook for 15 minutes, stirring.

3 Add the bouillon and milk, then bring the soup to a boil. Reduce the heat and let simmer for 45 minutes. Season to taste with salt and pepper.

4 Blend in the cream and let simmer for 5 minutes. Stir in the chopped fresh parsley, then transfer the soup to a warmed tureen or individual bowls and serve with soda bread.

NUTRITION
Calories *97*; Sugars *1.8 g*; Protein *7.3 g*;
Carbohydrate *4.2 g*; Fat *2 g*; Saturates *3.3 g*

⭐ very easy
🕐 5 mins
🕐 1 hr 20 mins

 COOK'S TIP

Soda bread is not made with yeast as bread usually is. Instead it is made with baking soda as the raising agent. It can be made with all-purpose flour or whole-wheat flour.

This creamy soup is filled with chunky vegetables and aromatic herbs. Using baby vegetables gives the soup an attractive look.

Chicken *and* Vegetable Soup

1 Put the bouillon into a pan with the chicken, parsley and tarragon sprigs, and garlic. Bring just to a boil, then reduce the heat, cover, and let simmer for 20 minutes or until the chicken is cooked through and firm to the touch.

2 Remove the chicken and strain the bouillon. When the chicken is cool enough to handle, cut into bite-size pieces.

3 Return the bouillon to the pan and bring to a boil. Adjust the heat so the liquid boils very gently. Add the carrots, cover, and cook for 5 minutes. Add the potatoes, cover again, and cook for about 12 minutes or until the vegetables are beginning to become tender.

4 Meanwhile, put the flour in a small mixing bowl and very slowly whisk in the milk to make a thick paste. Pour in a little of the hot bouillon mixture and stir to make a smooth liquid.

5 Stir the flour mixture into the soup and bring just to a boil, stirring. Boil gently for 4–5 minutes until it thickens, stirring frequently.

6 Add the scallions, asparagus, and chicken. Reduce the heat slightly and let simmer for about 15 minutes until all the vegetables are tender. Stir in the cream and herbs. Season to taste with salt and pepper and serve.

SERVES 4

4 cups chicken bouillon
6 oz/175 g skinless, boneless chicken breast
fresh parsley sprigs and tarragon sprigs
2 garlic cloves, crushed
4½ oz/125 g baby carrots, halved or cut
    into fourths
8 oz/225 g small new potatoes, quartered
4 tbsp all-purpose flour
½ cup milk
4–5 scallions, sliced diagonally
3 oz/85 g asparagus tips, halved and cut into
    1½-inch/4-cm pieces
½ cup whipping or heavy cream
1 tbsp finely chopped fresh parsley
1 tbsp finely chopped fresh tarragon
salt and pepper

NUTRITION
Calories 77; Sugars 1.5 g; Protein 5.5 g;
Carbohydrate 6.9 g; Fat 3.3 g; Saturates 1.9 g

⭐⭐   easy
🕐   5 mins
🕐   1 hr

Leek and potato soup is a classic recipe. Here the soup is enhanced with smoked bacon pieces and enriched with heavy cream for a little luxury.

Leek, Potato, *and* Bacon Soup

SERVES 4

2 tbsp butter
1 cup diced potatoes
4 leeks, shredded
2 garlic cloves, crushed
3½ oz/100 g smoked bacon, diced
3¾ cups vegetable bouillon
1 cup heavy cream
2 tbsp chopped fresh parsley
salt and pepper

to garnish
2 cups vegetable oil, for deep-frying
1 leek, shredded

1 Melt the butter in a large pan over low heat. Add the diced potatoes, shredded leeks, garlic, and diced bacon and sauté gently for 5 minutes, stirring constantly.

2 Add the bouillon and bring to a boil. Reduce the heat, cover the pan, and let simmer for 20 minutes until the potatoes are cooked. Stir in the cream and mix well.

3 Meanwhile, make the garnish. Half-fill a pan with vegetable oil and heat to 350–375°F/180–190°C or until a cube of bread browns in 30 seconds. Add the shredded leek and deep-fry for 1 minute until browned and crisp, taking care as it contains water. Drain the shredded leek thoroughly on paper towels and set aside.

4 Set aside a few pieces of potato, leek, and bacon. Put the rest of the soup into a food processor or blender, in batches, and process each batch for 30 seconds. Return the puréed soup to a clean pan and heat through.

5 Stir in the reserved vegetables, bacon, and parsley and season to taste with salt and pepper. Ladle into 4 warmed bowls and garnish with the fried leek.

NUTRITION
Calories *93*; Sugars *1 g*; Protein *3.3 g*;
Carbohydrate *2.7 g*; Fat *7.8 g*; Saturates *4.4 g*

easy

5 mins

30 mins

🍴 COOK'S TIP

For a lighter soup, omit the cream and stir yogurt or homemade crème fraîche into the soup at the end of the cooking time.

A comforting cold-weather soup, this is good served with bread as a main course, but it can also be an appetizer, served in smaller portions.

Lentil, Potato, *and* Ham Soup

1 Rinse and drain the lentils and pick over to check for any small stones.

2 Melt the butter in a large pan or flameproof casserole over medium heat. Add the onion, carrots, and garlic, then cover and cook for 4–5 minutes until the onion is slightly softened, stirring frequently.

3 Add the lentils to the vegetables with the water, bay leaf, and sage or rosemary. Bring to a boil, then reduce the heat, cover, and let simmer for 10 minutes.

4 Add the bouillon, potatoes, tomato paste and ham. Bring back to a simmer. Cover and continue simmering the soup for 25–30 minutes or until all the vegetables are tender.

5 Season to taste with salt and pepper, then remove and discard the bay leaf. Ladle into 4 warmed bowls, then garnish with parsley and serve.

SERVES 4

10½ oz/300 g Puy lentils
2 tsp butter
1 large onion, chopped finely
2 carrots, chopped finely
1 garlic clove, chopped finely
2 cups water
1 bay leaf
¼ tsp dried sage or rosemary
4 cups chicken bouillon
1⅓ cup diced potatoes
1 tbsp tomato paste
⅔ cup smoked ham, diced finely
salt and pepper
chopped fresh parsley, to garnish

NUTRITION
Calories 61; Sugars 1.4 g; Protein 5.4 g;
Carbohydrate 8.6 g; Fat 0.8 g; Saturates 0.3 g

⭐⭐   easy
          10 mins
          45–50 mins

This is a real winter warmer—pieces of tender beef and chunky mixed vegetables are cooked in a bouillon, which is flavored with sherry.

Chunky Potato *and* Beef Soup

SERVES 4

2 tbsp vegetable oil
8 oz/225 g lean frying steak, cut into strips
8 oz/225 g new potatoes, halved
1 carrot, diced
2 celery stalks, sliced
2 leeks, sliced
3¾ cups beef bouillon
8 baby corn cobs, sliced
1 bouquet garni
2 tbsp dry sherry
salt and pepper
chopped fresh parsley, to garnish

1 Heat the vegetable oil in a large pan over low heat.

2 Add the strips of meat to the pan and cook for 3 minutes, turning constantly.

3 Add the halved potatoes, diced carrot, sliced celery, and leeks. Cook for another 5 minutes, stirring.

4 Pour the beef bouillon into the pan and bring to a boil. Reduce the heat to a simmer, then add the sliced baby corn cobs and the bouquet garni.

5 Cook the soup for another 20 minutes or until cooked through.

6 Remove the bouquet garni from the pan. Stir the dry sherry into the soup and season to taste with salt and pepper.

7 Ladle the soup into warmed bowls and garnish with the chopped fresh parsley. Serve at once.

NUTRITION

Calories *187*; Sugars *3 g*; Protein *14 g*;
Carbohydrate *12 g*; Fat *9 g*; Saturates *2 g*

easy

5 mins

35 mins

🍲 COOK'S TIP

Make double the quantity of soup and freeze the remainder in a rigid container for later use. When ready to use, leave in the refrigerator to thaw thoroughly, then heat until piping hot.

A thick and hearty soup, nourishing and substantial enough to serve as an entrée with whole-wheat bread, if wished.

Indian Bean Soup

1 Heat the ghee or vegetable oil in a pan over medium heat. Add all the prepared vegetables, except the zucchini and green bell pepper, and cook, stirring frequently, for 5 minutes. Add the garlic, ground coriander, paprika, and curry paste and cook, stirring constantly, for 1 minute.

2 Stir in the bouillon and season with salt to taste. Bring to a boil, cover, and let simmer over low heat, stirring occasionally, for 25 minutes.

3 Stir in the black-eye peas, sliced zucchini, and green bell pepper, then replace the lid and continue cooking for another 15 minutes or until all the vegetables are tender.

4 Process 1¼ cups of the soup mixture (about 2 ladlefuls) in a food processor or blender. Return the puréed mixture to the soup in the pan and reheat until piping hot. Sprinkle with chopped cilantro (if using) and serve hot.

SERVES 6

4 tbsp ghee or vegetable oil
2 onions, chopped
8 oz/225 g potatoes, cut into chunks
8 oz/225 g parsnips, cut into chunks
8 oz/225 g turnips or rutabagas, cut into chunks
2 celery stalks, sliced
2 zucchini, sliced
1 green bell pepper, seeded and cut into ½-inch/1-cm pieces
2 garlic cloves, crushed
2 tsp ground coriander
1 tbsp paprika
1 tbsp mild curry paste
5 cups vegetable bouillon
salt
14 oz/400 g canned black-eye peas, drained and rinsed
chopped fresh cilantro, to garnish (optional)

NUTRITION
Calories 237; Sugars 9 g; Protein 9 g; Carbohydrate 33 g; Fat 9 g; Saturates 1 g

⭐⭐ easy
🕐 20 mins
🕐 50 mins

Potato skins are always a favorite. Prepare the skins in advance and warm them through before serving with the salad fillings.

Potato Skins *and* Two Fillings

SERVES 4

4 large baking potatoes
2 tbsp vegetable oil
4 tsp salt
fresh chives, to garnish
²/₃ cup sour cream, to serve

bean sprout filling

½ cup bean sprouts
1 celery stalk, sliced
1 orange, peeled and segmented
1 red eating apple, chopped
½ red bell pepper, chopped
1 tbsp chopped fresh parsley
1 tbsp light soy sauce
1 tbsp honey
1 small garlic clove, crushed

bean filling

1½ cups canned mixed beans, drained
1 onion, halved and sliced
1 tomato, chopped
2 scallions, chopped
2 tsp lemon juice
salt and pepper

NUTRITION

Calories *279*; Sugars *2 g*; Protein *5 g*;
Carbohydrate *44 g*; Fat *11 g*; Saturates *7 g*

   easy

30 mins

1 hr 10 mins

1 Scrub the potatoes and put onto a baking sheet. Prick the potatoes all over with a fork and rub the vegetable oil and salt into the skins.

2 Cook in a preheated oven, 400°F/200°C, for 1 hour or until softened.

3 Cut the potatoes in half lengthwise and scoop out the flesh, leaving a 1/2-inch/1-cm thick shell. Put the potato shells, skin side uppermost, into the oven for 10 minutes until crisp.

4 Mix the ingredients for the bean sprout filling in a bowl, then toss them in the soy sauce, honey, and garlic to coat.

5 Mix together the ingredients for the bean filling in a separate bowl.

6 Mix the sour cream and chives in another bowl.

7 Fill the potato skins with the 2 salad fillings and garnish with chopped fresh chives. Serve with the sour cream and chive sauce.

Use any mixture of beans you have to hand in this recipe, but the wider the variety, the more colorful the salad.

Mixed Bean *and* Apple Salad

1 Cook the potatoes in a pan of boiling water for 15 minutes until tender. Drain and transfer to a mixing bowl.

2 Add the mixed beans to the potatoes, with the apple, bell pepper, shallots, and fennel. Mix well, taking care not to break up the potatoes.

3 To make the dressing, whisk all the dressing ingredients together until thoroughly combined, then pour over the salad.

4 Line a serving plate or salad bowl with the oak-leaf lettuce leaves and spoon the salad mixture into the center. Serve at once.

SERVES 4

8 oz/225 g new potatoes, scrubbed and cut into fourths

8 oz/225 g mixed canned beans, such as red kidney beans, lima beans, and borlotti beans, drained and rinsed

1 red eating apple, diced and tossed in 1 tbsp lemon juice

1 yellow bell pepper, seeded and diced

1 shallot, sliced

½ fennel bulb, sliced

oak-leaf lettuce leaves

dressing

1 tbsp red wine vinegar

2 tbsp olive oil

½ tbsp mustard

1 garlic clove, crushed

2 tsp chopped fresh thyme

NUTRITION

Calories *183*; Sugars *8 g*; Protein *6 g*; Carbohydrate *26 g*; Fat *7 g*; Saturates *1 g*

⭐ very easy

🕐 20 mins

🕐 20 mins

COOK'S TIP

Use Dijon or whole-grain mustard in place of ordinary mustard, if you prefer.

The beets add a rich color to this dish. The dill dressing with the potato salad is a classic combination.

Beet Salad *and* Dill Dressing

SERVES 4

2²/₃ cups diced waxy potatoes
4 small cooked beets, sliced
½ small cucumber, sliced thinly
2 large dill pickles, sliced
1 red onion, halved and sliced
fresh dill sprigs, to garnish

dressing
1 garlic clove, crushed
2 tbsp olive oil
2 tbsp red wine vinegar
2 tbsp chopped fresh dill
salt and pepper

1 Cook the potatoes in a pan of boiling water for 15 minutes or until tender. Drain and let cool.

2 When cool, mix the potato and beets together in a bowl and set aside.

3 Line a salad platter with the slices of cucumber, dill pickles, and red onion.

4 Spoon the potato and beet mixture into the center of the platter.

5 Whisk all the dressing ingredients together in a small bowl, then pour the dressing over the salad.

6 Serve the potato and beet salad at once (see Cook's Tip), garnished with a few sprigs of fresh dill.

NUTRITION
Calories *174*; Sugars *8 g*; Protein *4 g*;
Carbohydrate *27 g*; Fat *6 g*; Saturates *1 g*

⭐ very easy
🕐 25 mins
🕐 15 mins

👨‍🍳 COOK'S TIP

If making the salad in advance, do not mix the beets and potatoes until just before serving, as the beet will bleed its color.

This hot, fruity salad combines sweet potato and fried bananas with colorful mixed bell peppers, tossed in a tasty honey-based dressing.

Sweet Potato Salad

1 Cook the sweet potatoes in a pan of boiling water for 10–15 minutes until tender. Drain thoroughly and set aside.

2 Meanwhile, melt the butter in a skillet over low heat. Add the lemon juice, garlic, and bell peppers and cook, stirring constantly, for 3 minutes.

3 Add the banana slices to the skillet and cook for 1 minute. Remove the bananas from the pan with a draining spoon and stir into the potatoes.

4 To make croutons, add the bread cubes to the skillet and cook, stirring frequently, for 2 minutes, until they are golden-brown on all sides.

5 Mix all of the dressing ingredients together in a small pan and heat until the honey is runny.

6 Spoon the potato mixture into a serving dish and season to taste with salt and pepper. Pour the dressing over the potatoes and sprinkle the croutons over the top. Serve at once.

SERVES 4

2³/₄ cups diced sweet potatoes
4 tbsp butter
1 tbsp lemon juice
1 garlic clove, crushed
1 red bell pepper, seeded and diced
1 green bell pepper, seeded and diced
2 bananas, sliced thickly
2 thick slices white bread, crusts removed, diced
salt and pepper

dressing
2 tbsp honey
2 tbsp chopped fresh chives
2 tbsp lemon juice
2 tbsp olive oil

NUTRITION
Calories *424*; Sugars *29 g*; Protein *5 g*; Carbohydrate *68 g*; Fat *17 g*; Saturates *8 g*

⭐⭐ easy

🕐 15 mins

🕐 20 mins

 COOK'S TIP

Use firm, slightly underripe bananas in this recipe because they won't turn soft and mushy when they are cooked.

There are many hot Indian-flavored potato dishes, which are served with curry, but this fruity salad is delicious chilled.

Indian Potato Salad

SERVES 4

generous 5 cups diced mealy potatoes
2³/₄ oz/75 g small broccoli florets
1 small mango, diced
4 scallions, sliced
salt and pepper
small cooked spiced poppadoms, to serve

dressing
½ tsp ground cumin
½ tsp ground coriander
1 tbsp mango chutney
²/₃ cup lowfat plain yogurt
1 tsp chopped fresh gingerroot
2 tbsp chopped fresh cilantro

1 Cook the potatoes in a pan of boiling water for 10 minutes or until tender. Drain and place in a mixing bowl.

2 Meanwhile, blanch the broccoli florets in a separate pan of boiling water for 2 minutes. Drain the broccoli well and add to the potatoes in the bowl.

3 When the potatoes and broccoli have cooled, add the diced mango and sliced scallions. Season to taste with salt and pepper and mix well.

4 Stir all of the dressing ingredients together in a small bowl.

5 Spoon the dressing over the potato mixture and mix together carefully, taking care not to break up the potatoes and broccoli.

6 Serve the salad at once with the spiced poppadoms.

NUTRITION
Calories *175*; Sugars *8 g*; Protein *6 g*;
Carbohydrate *38 g*; Fat *1 g*; Saturates *0.3 g*

 easy

25 mins

20 mins

🍳 **COOK'S TIP**

Mix the dressing ingredients together in advance and let chill in the refrigerator for a few hours for a stronger flavor to develop.

Crisp fried potato nests are perfect as an edible salad bowl and delicious when filled with a colorful Chinese-style salad of vegetables and fruit.

Nests *of* Chinese Salad

1 To make the nests, rinse the grated potatoes several times in cold water. Drain well on paper towels so they are completely dry. This is to prevent the potatoes spitting when they are cooked in the fat. Place the potatoes in a mixing bowl. Add the cornstarch and mix well to coat.

2 Half fill a preheated wok with vegetable oil and heat until smoking. Line a 6-inch/15-cm diameter wire strainer with one quarter of the potato mixture and press another strainer of the same size on top.

3 Carefully lower the strainers into the oil and cook for 2 minutes until the potato nest is golden-brown and crisp. Remove the strainers from the wok, allowing the excess oil to drain off.

4 Repeat 3 more times to use up all of the grated potato mixture and make a total of 4 nests. Let cool.

5 Mix the salad ingredients together, then spoon into the potato nests.

6 Mix the dressing ingredients together. Pour the dressing over the salad. Garnish with chives and then serve at once.

SERVES 4

potato nests
2¼ cups grated mealy potatoes
1 cup cornstarch
2 cups vegetable oil, for deep-frying
fresh chives, to garnish

salad
4½ oz/125 g pineapple, cubed
1 green bell pepper, cut into strips
1 carrot, cut into thin strips
1¾ oz/50 g snow peas, sliced thickly
4 baby corn cobs, halved lengthwise
¼ cup bean sprouts
2 scallions, sliced

dressing
1 tbsp honey
1 tsp light soy sauce
1 garlic clove, crushed
1 tsp lemon juice

NUTRITION
Calories *272*; Sugars *11 g*; Protein *4 g*;
Carbohydrate *59 g*; Fat *4 g*; Saturates *0.4 g*

✪✪✪ moderate
🕐 15 mins
🕐 15 mins

This green and white salad is made with creamy, salty-flavored goat cheese—its distinctive flavor is perfect with salad leaves.

Arugula *and* Apple Salad

SERVES 4

1 lb 5 oz/600 g potatoes, unpeeled and sliced
2 green eating apples, diced
1 tsp lemon juice
1 oz/25 g walnut pieces
4½ oz/125 g goat cheese, cubed
5½ oz/150 g arugula leaves
salt and pepper

dressing
2 tbsp olive oil
1 tbsp red wine vinegar
1 tsp honey
1 tsp fennel seeds

1 Cook the potatoes in a pan of boiling water for 15 minutes until tender. Drain and let cool. Transfer the cooled potatoes to a serving bowl.

2 Toss the diced apples in the lemon juice, then drain and stir them into the cold potatoes.

3 Add the walnut pieces, goat cheese cubes, and arugula leaves, then toss the salad to mix. Season to taste with salt and pepper.

4 Whisk the dressing ingredients together in a small bowl and then pour the dressing over the salad. Serve the salad at once.

NUTRITION
Calories *104*; Sugars *3.1 g*; Protein *3.1 g*;
Carbohydrate *12 g*; Fat *5.3 g*; Saturates *1.5 g*

easy
20 mins
15 mins

🍳 **COOK'S TIP**

Serve at once to prevent the apple from discoloring. Alternatively, prepare all of the other ingredients in advance and add the apple at the last minute.

Broiled new potatoes are tossed in oil for a charbroiled flavor and color. Served warm with a garlic mayonnaise, they make a delicious salad.

Broiled New Potato Salad

1 Cook the new potatoes in a pan of boiling water for 10 minutes. Drain.

2 Mix the olive oil, thyme, and paprika together and pour the mixture over the warm potatoes.

3 Place the bacon slices under a preheated medium–hot broiler and cook for 5 minutes, turning once until crisp. When cooked, coarsely chop the bacon and keep warm while you broil the potatoes.

4 Transfer the potatoes to the broiler pan. Cook for 10 minutes, turning once.

5 Mix the dressing ingredients together in a small bowl. Transfer the potatoes and bacon to a large serving bowl. Season to taste with salt and pepper and mix well.

6 Spoon over the dressing, garnish with a parsley sprig and serve at once. Alternatively, let cool and serve chilled.

SERVES 4

1 lb 8 oz/675 g new potatoes, scrubbed
3 tbsp olive oil
2 tbsp chopped fresh thyme
1 tsp paprika
4 smoked bacon slices
salt and pepper
fresh parsley sprig, to garnish

dressing
4 tbsp mayonnaise
1 tbsp garlic wine vinegar
2 garlic cloves, crushed
1 tbsp chopped fresh parsley

NUTRITION
Calories *162*; Sugars *1 g*; Protein *3.2 g*;
Carbohydrate *12 g*; Fat *11.4 g*; Saturates *2.2 g*

easy

5 mins

25 mins

COOK'S TIP

Add spicy sausage to the salad instead of bacon—you do not need to cook it under the broiler before adding it to the salad.

This is a classic version of the French Salade Niçoise. It is a substantial salad, suitable for a lunch or light summer supper.

Tuna Niçoise Salad

SERVES 4

4 eggs
1 lb/450 g new potatoes
1 cup small green beans, trimmed and halved
2 tuna steaks, about 6 oz/175 g each
6 tbsp olive oil, plus extra for brushing
1 garlic clove, crushed
1½ tsp Dijon mustard
2 tsp lemon juice
2 tbsp chopped fresh basil
2 Boston lettuces
1½ cups cherry tomatoes, halved
2 cups, peeled and sliced cucumber
½ cup pitted black olives
1¾ oz/50 g canned anchovy fillets in oil, drained
salt and pepper

NUTRITION
Calories 109; Sugars 1 g; Protein 7 g;
Carbohydrate 4.8 g; Fat 7 g; Saturates 1.2 g

⭐ very easy
🕐 10 mins
🕐 20 mins

1 Bring a small pan of water to a boil over medium heat. Add the eggs and then cook for 7–9 minutes from when the water returns to a boil—7 minutes for a slightly soft center, 9 minutes for a firm center. Drain and refresh under cold running water. Set the hard-cooked eggs aside.

2 Cook the potatoes in boiling salted water for 10–12 minutes until tender. Add the green beans 3 minutes before the end of the cooking time. Drain both vegetables well and refresh under cold running water. Drain well.

3 Wash the tuna steaks under cold running water and pat dry with paper towels. Brush with a little olive oil and season to taste with salt and pepper. Cook on a preheated ridged griddle for 2–3 minutes on each side until just tender, but still slightly pink in the center. Set aside.

4 Whisk the garlic, mustard, lemon juice, basil, and seasoning together. Whisk the olive oil into the dressing.

5 To assemble the salad, break apart the lettuces and tear into large pieces. Divide among individual plates. Add the potatoes and beans, tomatoes, cucumber, and olives. Toss lightly. Shell the eggs and cut into fourths lengthwise. Arrange these on top of the salad. Sprinkle over the anchovies.

6 Flake the tuna and arrange on the salads. Pour over the dressing and serve.

The spicy peanut dressing served with this salad may be prepared in advance and left to chill a day before required.

Indonesian Chicken Salad

1 Using a sharp knife, carefully cut the potatoes into small dice. Bring a large pan of water to the boil over medium heat.

2 Cook the diced potatoes in the boiling water for 10 minutes or until tender. Drain them and let cool until required.

3 Transfer the cooled potatoes to a salad bowl.

4 Add the pineapple, carrots, bean sprouts, scallions, zucchini, celery, peanuts, and sliced chicken to the potatoes. Toss well to mix all the ingredients.

5 To make the dressing, put the peanut butter in a small mixing bowl and gradually whisk in the olive oil and light soy sauce.

6 Stir in the chopped red chile, sesame oil, and lime juice. Mix well.

7 Pour the spicy dressing over the salad and toss lightly to coat all of the ingredients. Serve the potato and chicken salad at once.

SERVES 4

2 lb 12 oz/1.25 kg waxy potatoes
10½ oz/300 g fresh pineapple, diced
2 carrots, grated
1¾ cups bean sprouts
1 bunch of scallions, sliced
1 large zucchini, cut into thin sticks
3 celery stalks, cut into thin sticks
6 oz/175 g unsalted peanuts
2 cooked chicken breast fillets, about
　4½ oz/125 g each, sliced

dressing
6 tbsp crunchy peanut butter
6 tbsp olive oil
2 tbsp light soy sauce
1 fresh red chile, chopped
2 tsp sesame oil
4 tsp lime juice

NUTRITION
Calories *802*; Sugars *15 g*; Protein *35 g*;
Carbohydrate *45 g*; Fat *55 g*; Saturates *10 g*

⭐⭐　　　　easy

🕐　　　　20 mins

🕐　　　　15 mins

🍳 COOK'S TIP

Unsweetened canned pineapple may be used instead of the fresh pineapple for convenience. If only sweetened canned pineapple is available, drain it and rinse under cold running water before using.

Tender chicken breast meat is perfect for salads. It cooks quickly in small pieces and these are perfect for tossing with other salad ingredients.

Spicy Chicken Salad

S E R V E S   4

2 skinned chicken breast fillets, about
   4¹⁄₂ oz/125 g each
2 tbsp butter
1 fresh red chile, chopped
1 tbsp honey
¹⁄₂ tsp ground cumin
2 tbsp chopped fresh cilantro
3¹⁄₂ cups diced potatoes
1³⁄₄ oz/50 g green beans, halved
1 red bell pepper, cut into thin strips
2 tomatoes, seeded and diced

dressing
2 tbsp olive oil
pinch of chili powder
1 tbsp garlic wine vinegar
pinch of superfine sugar
1 tbsp chopped fresh cilantro

1 Cut the chicken into thin strips. Melt the butter in a pan over medium heat. Add the chicken, chile, honey, and cumin and cook for 10 minutes, turning until cooked through.

2 Transfer the mixture to a bowl and let cool, then stir in the cilantro.

3 Meanwhile, cook the diced potatoes in a pan of boiling water for 10 minutes until they are tender. Drain and let cool.

4 Blanch the green beans in a pan of boiling water for 3 minutes. Drain and let cool. Mix the green beans and potatoes together in a salad bowl.

5 Add the bell pepper strips and the diced tomatoes to the potatoes and green beans. Stir in the spicy chicken mixture.

6 Whisk the dressing ingredients together in a small bowl and pour the dressing over the salad, tossing well. Serve the salad at once.

N U T R I T I O N
Calories *105*; Sugars *2.8 g*; Protein *6.7 g*;
Carbohydrate *9.2 g*; Fat *5 g*; Saturates *1.8 g*

easy

20 mins

15 mins

COOK'S TIP

If you prefer, use lean turkey meat instead of the chicken for a slightly stronger flavor. Use the white meat for the best appearance and flavor.

Sliced Italian sausage blends well with the other Mediterranean flavors of sun-dried tomato and basil in this salad.

Italian Sausage Salad

1 Cook the potatoes in a pan of boiling water for 20 minutes or until cooked through. Drain and let cool.

2 Line a large serving platter with the radicchio or other red lettuce leaves.

3 Slice the cooled potatoes and arrange them in layers on the lettuce-lined serving platter together with the sliced green bell pepper, sliced Italian sausage, red onion, sun-dried tomatoes, and shredded fresh basil.

4 Whisk the balsamic vinegar, tomato paste, and olive oil together in a small bowl and season to taste with salt and pepper. Pour the dressing over the potato salad and serve at once.

SERVES 4

1 lb/450 g waxy potatoes
1 radicchio or other red lettuce
1 green bell pepper, sliced
6 oz/175 g Italian sausage, sliced
1 red onion, halved and sliced
4½ oz/125 g sun-dried tomatoes, sliced
2 tbsp shredded fresh basil

dressing
1 tbsp balsamic vinegar
1 tsp tomato paste
2 tbsp olive oil
salt and pepper

NUTRITION
Calories *450*; Sugars *6 g*; Protein *13 g*;
Carbohydrate *38 g*; Fat *28 g*; Saturates *1 g*

easy
25 mins
25 mins

COOK'S TIP

Any sliced Italian sausage or salami can be used in this salad. Italy is home of the salami and there are numerous varieties to choose from—those from the south tend to be more highly spiced than those from the north of the country.

Light Meals *and* Side Dishes

Potatoes are very versatile and can be used as a base to create an array of tempting light meals and satisfying snacks. They are also nutritious, and their carbohydrate gives a welcome energy boost. Because potatoes have a fairly neutral flavor, they can be teamed with a variety of other ingredients and flavors.

This chapter contains a range of delicious yet light meals—try Feta & Spinach Omelet, or Carrot & Potato Soufflé. Potatoes can be cooked in a variety of ways, such as mashing, roasting, deep-frying, and baking, making them an adaptable component of any meal.

These twice-baked
potatoes have an unusual
filling made from the
Middle Eastern flavors of
garbanzo beans, cumin,
and cilantro.

Potatoes *with a* Spicy Filling

SERVES 4

4 large baking potatoes
1 tbsp vegetable oil, optional
15½ oz/425 g canned garbanzo
   beans, drained
1 tsp ground coriander
1 tsp ground cumin
4 tbsp fresh cilantro, chopped
⅔ cup lowfat plain yogurt
salt and pepper

salad

2 tomatoes
½ cucumber
½ red onion
4 tbsp chopped fresh cilantro

1 Scrub the potatoes and pat them dry with paper towels. Prick the potatoes all over with a fork. Brush with oil (if using) and season with salt and pepper.

2 Place the potatoes on a large cookie sheet and bake in a preheated oven, 400°F/200°C, for 1–1¼ hours or until cooked through. Let cool for 10 minutes.

3 Mash the garbanzo beans in a large mixing bowl. Stir in the ground coriander, cumin, and half the cilantro. Cover with plastic wrap and set aside.

4 Halve the cooked potatoes and scoop the flesh into a bowl, keeping the shells intact. Mash the flesh until smooth and gently mix into the garbanzo mixture with the yogurt. Season to taste with salt and pepper.

5 Place the potato shells on a cookie sheet and fill with the potato and garbanzo bean mixture. Return the potatoes to the oven and bake for about 10–15 minutes until heated through.

6 Meanwhile, make the salad. Using a sharp knife, chop the tomatoes. Slice the cucumber and cut the red onion into thin slices. Toss all the ingredients together with the cilantro in a serving dish.

7 Serve the potatoes sprinkled with the remaining cilantro and the salad.

NUTRITION
Calories *335*; Sugars *7 g*; Protein *15 g*;
Carbohydrate *57 g*; Fat *7 g*; Saturates *1 g*

⭐ very easy
   20 mins
   1 hr 30 mins

These Indian snacks are perfect for a quick or light meal. Served with a salad, they can be made in advance and frozen.

Vegetable Samosas

1 To make the filling, heat the vegetable oil in a skillet over low heat. Add the onion and sauté, stirring frequently, for 1–2 minutes until softened. Stir in all of the spices and garlic and cook for 1 minute.

2 Add the potatoes and cook over low heat, stirring frequently, for 5 minutes, until they begin to soften.

3 Stir in the peas and spinach and cook for another 3–4 minutes.

4 Lay the phyllo pastry sheets out on a clean counter and carefully fold 12 sheets in half lengthwise.

5 Place 2 tablespoons of the vegetable filling at one end of each folded pastry sheet. Fold over one corner to make a triangle. Continue folding in this way to make a triangular package and seal the edges with water.

6 Repeat with the remaining pastry and the remaining filling.

7 Heat the vegetable oil for deep-frying in a large pan or deep-fryer to 350°F/180°C, or until a cube of bread browns in 30 seconds. Add the samosas, in batches, and fry for 1–2 minutes until golden. Drain on paper towels and keep warm while cooking the remainder. Serve the vegetable samosas immediately.

MAKES 12

filling
2 tbsp vegetable oil
1 onion, chopped
½ tsp ground coriander
½ tsp ground cumin
pinch of turmeric
½ tsp ground ginger
½ tsp garam masala
1 garlic clove, crushed
1½ cups diced potatoes
1 cup frozen peas, thawed
5½ oz/150 g fresh spinach, chopped

pastry
12 oz/350 g phyllo pastry
2 cups vegetable oil, for deep-frying

NUTRITION
Calories *291*; Sugars *2 g*; Protein *4 g*;
Carbohydrate *18 g*; Fat *23 g*; Saturates *3 g*

✪✪✪   moderate
🕐   20 mins
🕐   30 mins

These gnocchi or small dumplings are made with potato and flavored with spinach and nutmeg, then served in a tomato and basil sauce.

Gnocchi *with* Tomato Sauce

SERVES 4

1 lb/450 g baking potatoes
2¾ oz/75 g spinach
1 tsp water
3 tbsp butter or margarine
1 small egg, beaten
¾ cup all-purpose flour, plus extra for dusting
salt and pepper
fresh basil leaves, to garnish

tomato sauce

1 tbsp olive oil
1 shallot, chopped
1 tbsp tomato paste
8 oz/225 g canned chopped tomatoes
2 tbsp chopped fresh basil
6 tbsp red wine
1 tsp superfine sugar

NUTRITION

Calories *337*; Sugars *4 g*; Protein *9 g*; Carbohydrate *52 g*; Fat *10 g*; Saturates *4 g*

⭐⭐⭐   moderate
🕐   25 mins
🕐   1 hr

1 Cook the potatoes in their skins in a large pan of boiling salted water for 20 minutes. Drain well and press through a strainer into a bowl.

2 Cook the spinach in the water for 5 minutes or until wilted. Drain and pat dry with paper towels. Chop and stir into the potatoes.

3 Add the butter or margarine, egg, and half of the flour to the spinach mixture, mixing well. Turn out onto a floured counter, gradually kneading in the remaining flour to form a soft dough.

4 With floured hands, roll the dough into thin ropes and cut off ¾-inch/2-cm pieces. Press the center of each dumpling with your finger, drawing it toward you to curl the sides of the gnocchi. Cover the gnocchi and let chill.

5 Heat the olive oil for the sauce in a pan over low heat. Add the chopped shallots and sauté for 5 minutes. Add the tomato paste, tomatoes, basil, red wine, and sugar and season well with salt and pepper. Bring to a boil and then let simmer for 20 minutes.

6 Bring a pan of lightly salted water to a boil over medium heat. Add the gnocchi and cook for 2–3 minutes or until they rise to the top of the pan. Drain well and transfer to serving dishes. Spoon the tomato sauce over the gnocchi. Garnish with basil and serve.

These spicy vegetable burgers are delicious, especially when served in a warm bun or roll with light oven fries.

Vegetable Burgers *and* Fries

1 To make the burgers, cook the spinach in a little boiling water for about 2 minutes. Drain thoroughly and pat dry with paper towels.

2 Heat the olive oil in a skillet over low heat. Add the leek and garlic and sauté for 2–3 minutes. Add the mushrooms, bean curd, spices, and cilantro, and cook for 5–7 minutes until the vegetables have softened. Toss in the spinach and cook for 1 minute.

3 Transfer the mixture to a food processor and process for 30 seconds until almost smooth. Transfer to a bowl and stir in the bread crumbs, mixing well. Let stand until cool enough to handle. Using floured hands, form the mixture equally into 4 burgers. Let chill for 30 minutes.

4 To make the fries, cut the potatoes into thin wedges and cook in a pan of boiling water for 10 minutes. Drain and toss in the flour and chili powder. Lay the fries on a cookie sheet and sprinkle with the olive oil. Cook in a preheated oven, 400°F/200°C, for 30 minutes or until golden.

5 Meanwhile, heat the remaining oil in a skillet and cook the burgers for about 8–10 minutes, turning once. Serve with salad greens in a bun or roll with the fries.

SERVES 4

vegetable burgers
3½ oz/100 g spinach
1 tbsp olive oil
1 leek, chopped
2 garlic cloves, crushed
1½ cups chopped mushrooms
10½ oz/300 g firm bean curd, chopped
1 tsp chili powder
1 tsp curry powder
1 tbsp chopped fresh cilantro
1½ cups fresh whole-wheat bread crumbs
1 tbsp olive oil
burger buns or rolls and salad, to serve

fries
2 large potatoes
2 tbsp flour
1 tsp chili powder
2 tbsp olive oil

NUTRITION
Calories *416*; Sugars *4 g*; Protein *18 g*;
Carbohydrate *64 g*; Fat *17 g*; Saturates *2 g*

⭐⭐⭐   moderate
🕐   45 mins
🕐   1 hr

This pâté is easy to prepare and may be stored in the refrigerator for up to two days. Serve with small toasts, Melba toast, or a selection of crudités.

Potato *and* Bean Pâté

SERVES 4

²/₃ cup mealy potatoes, diced
8 oz/225 g mixed canned beans, such as
   borlotti beans, lima beans, and kidney
   beans, drained
1 garlic clove, crushed
2 tsp lime juice
1 tbsp chopped fresh cilantro
2 tbsp plain unsweetened yogurt
salt and pepper
chopped fresh cilantro, to garnish

1 Cook the potatoes in a pan of boiling water for 10 minutes until tender. Drain well and mash thoroughly until smooth.

2 Transfer the potato to a food processor or blender and add the beans, garlic, lime juice, and the fresh cilantro. Season to taste with salt and pepper and process for 1 minute until a smooth purée forms. Alternatively, mix the beans with the potato, garlic, lime juice, and cilantro and mash well by hand.

3 Turn the pâté into a bowl and add the yogurt. Mix well.

4 Spoon the pâté into a serving dish and garnish with the chopped cilantro. Serve at once or cover with plastic wrap and let chill before use.

NUTRITION
Calories *84*; Sugars *3 g*; Protein *5 g*;
Carbohydrate *16 g*; Fat *0.5 g*; Saturates *0.1 g*

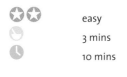

easy

3 mins

10 mins

🍳 COOK'S TIP

For Melba toast, toast sliced bread lightly on both sides under a preheated high broiler. Remove the crusts. Holding it flat, slide a sharp knife through the slice to split it horizontally. Cut into triangles and toast the untoasted sides.

These cakes will be loved by vegetarians and meat-eaters alike, packed with creamy potato and a wide a variety of mushrooms.

Mixed Mushroom Cakes

1 Cook the potatoes in a pan of lightly salted boiling water for 10 minutes, or until cooked through.

2 Drain the potatoes well. Mash with a potato masher or fork and set aside.

3 Meanwhile, melt the butter in a skillet over low heat. Add the mushrooms and garlic and cook, stirring constantly, for 5 minutes. Drain well.

4 Stir the mushrooms and garlic into the potato, together with the beaten egg and chives.

5 Divide the mixture equally into 4 portions and form them into round cakes. Toss them in the flour until the outsides of the cakes are completely coated.

6 Heat the vegetable oil in a skillet over medium heat. Add the potato cakes and cook for 10 minutes until golden-brown, turning them over halfway through. Garnish with fresh chives and serve the cakes at once, with crisp salad greens.

SERVES 4

2¾ cups diced mealy potatoes
2 tbsp butter
6 oz/175 g mixed mushrooms, chopped
2 garlic cloves, crushed
1 small egg, beaten
1 tbsp chopped fresh chives
all-purpose flour, for dusting
2 cups vegetable oil, for frying
salt and pepper
handful of fresh chives, to garnish
salad greens, to serve

NUTRITION
Calories 298; Sugars 0.8 g; Protein 5 g; Carbohydrate 22 g; Fat 22 g; Saturates 5 g

⭐⭐ easy
🕐 20 mins
🕐 25 mins

🧑‍🍳 COOK'S TIP

Prepare the cakes in advance: cover and let chill in the refrigerator for up to 24 hours, if you wish.

These grated potato cakes are also known as straw cakes, as they resemble a straw mat! Serve with a tomato sauce or salad.

Cheese *and* Onion Rösti

SERVES 4

2 lb/900 g potatoes
1 onion, grated
½ cup grated Swiss cheese
2 tbsp chopped fresh parsley
1 tbsp olive oil
2 tbsp butter
salt and pepper

to garnish
1 scallion shredded
1 small tomato, cut into fourths

1 Parboil the potatoes in a pan of lightly salted boiling water for 10 minutes and let cool. Peel the potatoes and grate with a coarse grater. Place the grated potatoes in a large mixing bowl.

2 Stir in the onion, cheese, and parsley. Season to taste with salt and pepper. Divide the potato mixture equally into 4 portions and form into cakes.

3 Heat half of the olive oil and butter in a skillet over high heat. Add 2 of the potato cakes and cook for 1 minute, then reduce the heat and cook for 5 minutes until they are golden underneath. Turn the potato cakes over and cook them for another 5 minutes.

4 Repeat with the other half of the oil and the remaining butter to cook the remaining 2 cakes. Transfer to warmed individual serving plates. Garnish with shredded scallion and tomato fourths and serve immediately.

NUTRITION

Calories *307*; Sugars *4 g*; Protein *8 g*;
Carbohydrate *42 g*; Fat *13 g*; Saturates *6 g*

easy

10 mins

40 mins

🍳 COOK'S TIP

The potato cakes should be flattened as much as possible during cooking, otherwise the outside will be cooked before the center.

These fritters make a filling snack. They are an excellent way to use up leftover cooked vegetables.

Potato *and* Cauliflower Fritters

1 Cook the potatoes in a pan of boiling water for 10 minutes until cooked through. Drain well and mash.

2 Meanwhile, cook the cauliflower florets in a separate pan of boiling water for 10 minutes. Drain thoroughly.

3 Mix the cauliflower florets into the mashed potato. Stir in the grated Parmesan cheese and season well with salt and pepper.

4 Separate the whole egg and beat the yolk into the potato and cauliflower.

5 Lightly whisk both the egg whites in a clean bowl, then carefully fold into the potato and cauliflower mixture.

6 Divide the potato and cauliflower mixture equally into 8 portions and form them into rounds.

7 Heat the vegetable oil in a skillet over medium heat. Add the fritters and cook for 3–5 minutes, turning once halfway through cooking.

8 Dust the cooked fritters with a little paprika, if wished, and serve at once accompanied by crisp-fried bacon.

SERVES 4

1½ cups diced mealy potatoes
8 oz/225 g cauliflower florets
scant ½ cup freshly grated Parmesan cheese
1 egg, plus 1 extra egg white
3–4 tbsp vegetable oil, for frying
paprika, for dusting (optional)
salt and pepper
crisp-fried bacon slices, chopped, to serve

NUTRITION
Calories *665*; Sugars *5 g*; Protein *18 g*;
Carbohydrate *98 g*; Fat *25 g*; Saturates *4 g*

⭐⭐⭐   moderate
🕐   10 mins
🕐   15–20 mins

🍳 **COOK'S TIP**

Any other vegetable, such as broccoli, can be used in this recipe instead of the cauliflower florets, if you prefer.

Chunks of cooked potato are coated first in Parmesan cheese, then in a light batter, before being fried until golden for a delicious hot snack.

Fritters *with* Garlic Sauce

SERVES 4

1 lb 2 oz/500 g waxy potatoes, cubed
1¼ cups freshly grated Parmesan cheese
2 cups vegetable oil, for deep-frying

sauce
2 tbsp butter
1 onion, halved and sliced
2 garlic cloves, crushed
¼ cup all-purpose flour
1¼ cups milk
1 tbsp chopped fresh parsley

batter
½ cup all-purpose flour
1 small egg
⅔ cup milk

1 To make the sauce, melt the butter in a pan over low heat. Add the sliced onion and garlic and cook, stirring frequently, for 2–3 minutes. Add the flour and cook, stirring constantly, for 1 minute.

2 Remove from the heat and stir in the milk and parsley. Return to the heat and bring to a boil. Keep warm.

3 Meanwhile, cook the cubed potatoes in a pan of boiling water for about 5–10 minutes until just firm. Do not overcook or they will fall apart.

4 Drain the potatoes and toss them in the Parmesan cheese. If the potatoes are still slightly wet, the cheese sticks to them better and coats them well.

5 To make the batter, place the flour in a mixing bowl and gradually beat in the egg and milk until smooth. Dip the potato cubes into the batter to coat.

6 Heat the oil in a large pan to 350°F/180°C, or until a cube of bread browns in 30 seconds. Add the fritters and cook for 3–4 minutes or until golden.

7 Remove the fritters with a draining spoon and drain well. Transfer them to a warmed serving bowl and serve immediately with the garlic sauce.

NUTRITION
Calories 599; Sugars 9 g; Protein 22 g;
Carbohydrate 42 g; Fat 39 g; Saturates 13 g

easy
20 mins
20–25 mins

This quick, chunky omelet has pieces of potato cooked into the egg mixture and is then filled with feta cheese and baby spinach.

Feta *and* Spinach Omelet

1 Heat 2 tablespoons of the butter in a skillet over low heat. Add the potatoes and cook, stirring constantly, for 7–10 minutes until golden. Transfer to a bowl and set aside.

2 Add the garlic, paprika, and tomatoes to the pan with the potatoes and cook for another 2 minutes.

3 Whisk the eggs together and season with pepper. Pour the eggs into the potatoes and mix well.

4 Cook the spinach in a pan of boiling water for 1 minute until just wilted. Drain and refresh under cold running water. Pat dry with paper towels. Stir in the fennel seeds, feta cheese, and yogurt.

5 Heat one quarter of the remaining butter in a 6-inch/15-cm omelet pan. Ladle one quarter of the egg and potato mixture into the pan. Cook, turning once, for 2 minutes until the omelet sets.

6 Spoon one quarter of the spinach mixture onto one half of the omelet, then fold the omelet in half over the filling. Transfer the omelet to a serving plate. Repeat to make 4 omelets.

SERVES 4

6 tbsp butter
8 cups waxy potatoes, diced
3 garlic cloves, crushed
1 tsp paprika
2 tomatoes, peeled, seeded, and diced
12 eggs
pepper

filling

8 oz/225 g baby spinach
1 tsp fennel seeds
4½ oz/125 g feta cheese, diced
4 tbsp plain unsweetened yogurt

NUTRITION
Calories *564*; Sugars *6 g*; Protein *30 g*;
Carbohydrate *25 g*; Fat *39 g*; Saturates *19 g*

easy
20 mins
25–30 mins

🍳 **COOK'S TIP**

Use any other cheese, such as blue cheese, instead of the feta, and blanched broccoli in place of the baby spinach, if you prefer.

These oven-baked mushrooms are covered with a creamy potato and mushroom filling, topped with melted cheese.

Creamy Stuffed Mushrooms

SERVES 4

1 oz/25 g dried ceps
1½ cups diced mealy potatoes
2 tbsp butter, melted
4 tbsp heavy cream
2 tbsp chopped fresh chives
8 large open-cup mushrooms
¼ cup grated Emmenthal cheese
⅔ cup vegetable bouillon
salt and pepper
fresh chives, to garnish
salad greens, to serve

1 Place the dried ceps in a small bowl. Add enough boiling water to cover and let soak for 20 minutes.

2 Meanwhile, cook the potatoes in a medium pan of lightly salted boiling water for 10 minutes until cooked through and tender. Drain well and mash thoroughly until smooth.

3 Drain the soaked ceps and then chop them finely. Mix the chopped ceps into the mashed potato.

4 Blend the butter, cream, and chives together and pour the mixture into the cep and potato mixture, mixing well. Season to taste with salt and pepper.

5 Remove the stems from the open-cup mushrooms. Chop the stems and stir them into the potato mixture. Spoon the mixture into the mushrooms and sprinkle the cheese over the top.

6 Arrange the filled mushrooms in a shallow ovenproof dish and pour in the vegetable bouillon. Cover the dish with a lid or foil. Cook in a preheated oven, 425°F/220°C, for 20 minutes. Remove the lid and cook for 5 more minutes. Transfer to a serving plate, garnish with chives and serve with salad greens.

NUTRITION

Calories 214; Sugars 1 g; Protein 5 g;
Carbohydrate 11 g; Fat 17 g; Saturates 11 g

easy

40 mins

40 mins

🍲 COOK'S TIP

Use fresh mushrooms instead of the dried ceps, if preferred, and stir a mixture of chopped nuts into the mushroom stuffing mixture for extra crunch.

Use any mixture of mushrooms to hand for this creamy layered bake. It can be served straight from the dish in which it is cooked.

Potato *and* Mushroom Bake

1 Grease a shallow round ovenproof dish with butter.

2 Parboil the sliced potatoes in a pan of boiling water for 10 minutes. Drain well. Layer one quarter of the potatoes in the base of the dish.

3 Arrange one quarter of the mushrooms on top of the potatoes and sprinkle with one quarter of the rosemary, chives, and garlic. Continue making layers in the same order, finishing with a layer of potatoes on top.

4 Pour the cream over the top of the potatoes, then season to taste with salt and pepper.

5 Cook in a preheated oven, 375°F/190°C, for about 45 minutes or until the bake is golden-brown and piping hot.

6 Garnish with chopped chives and serve at once straight from the dish.

SERVES 4

2 tbsp butter
1 lb 2 oz/500 g waxy potatoes, sliced thinly
2 cups sliced mixed mushrooms
1 tbsp chopped fresh rosemary
4 tbsp chopped fresh chives
2 garlic cloves, crushed
2/3 cup heavy cream
salt and pepper
chopped fresh chives, to garnish

NUTRITION
Calories 304; Sugars 2 g; Protein 4 g; Carbohydrate 20 g; Fat 24 g; Saturates 15 g

easy

15 mins

55 mins

🍳 COOK'S TIP

For a special occasion, the bake may be made in a lined cake pan and then turned out to serve.

This is a filling Indian sandwich. Spicy potatoes fill the nan breads, which are served with a cool cucumber raita and lime pickle on the side.

Potato-Filled Nan Breads

SERVES 4

1½ cups scrubbed and diced waxy potatoes
1 tbsp vegetable oil
1 onion, chopped
2 garlic cloves, crushed
1 tsp ground cumin
1 tsp ground coriander
½ tsp chili powder
1 tbsp tomato paste
3 tbsp vegetable bouillon
2¾ oz/75 g baby spinach, shredded
4 small or 2 large nan breads
lime pickle, to serve

raita
⅔ cup lowfat plain yogurt
4 tbsp diced cucumber
1 tbsp chopped fresh mint

1 Cook the diced potatoes in a pan of boiling water for 10 minutes. Drain thoroughly and set aside.

2 Heat the vegetable oil in a separate pan over medium–low heat. Add the onion and garlic and cook for 3 minutes, stirring. Add the spices and cook for another 2 minutes.

3 Stir in the potatoes, tomato paste, vegetable bouillon, and spinach. Cook for 5 minutes until the potatoes are tender.

4 Warm the nan breads in a preheated oven, 300°F/150°C, for about 2 minutes.

5 To make the raita, mix the yogurt, cucumber, and mint in a small bowl.

6 Remove the nan breads from the oven. Using a sharp knife, cut a pocket in the side of each nan bread. Spoon the potato mixture into each pocket.

7 Serve the filled nan breads at once, with the raita and lime pickle.

NUTRITION
Calories *244*; Sugars *7 g*; Protein *8 g*;
Carbohydrate *37 g*; Fat *8 g*; Saturates *1 g*

easy

10 mins

25 mins

🍳 **COOK'S TIP**

To give the raita a much stronger flavor, make it in advance and let chill in the refrigerator until ready to serve.

These small pasties are made with crisp phyllo pastry and filled with a tasty spinach and potato mixture flavored with chili and tomato.

Potato *and* Spinach Triangles

1 Lightly grease a baking sheet with a little butter.

2 Cook the potatoes in a pan of lightly salted boiling water for 10 minutes or until cooked through. Drain thoroughly and place in a mixing bowl.

3 Meanwhile, put the spinach in a pan with 2 tablespoonfuls of water. Cover and cook over low heat for 2 minutes until wilted. Drain the spinach thoroughly, squeezing out excess moisture, and add to the potato.

4 Stir in the chopped tomato, chili powder, and lemon juice. Season to taste with salt and pepper.

5 Lightly brush 8 sheets of phyllo pastry with melted butter. Spread out 4 of the sheets and lay the other 4 on top of each. Cut them into rectangles about 8 x 4 inches/20 x 10 cm.

6 Spoon the potato and spinach mixture on to one end of each rectangle. Fold a corner of the pastry over the filling, fold the pointed end back over the pastry strip, then fold over the remaining pastry to form a triangle.

7 Place the triangles on the baking sheet and bake in a preheated oven, 190°C/375°F, for 20 minutes or until golden-brown.

8 To make the lemon mayonnaise, mix the mayonnaise, lemon juice, and lemon rind together in a small bowl. Serve the potato and spinach triangles warm or cold with the lemon mayonnaise.

SERVES 4

2 tbsp butter, melted, plus extra for greasing
1½ cups finely diced waxy potatoes
1 lb 2 oz/500 g baby spinach
1 tomato, seeded and chopped
¼ tsp chili powder
½ tsp lemon juice
8 oz/225 g phyllo pastry, thawed if frozen
salt and pepper

lemon mayonnaise
⅔ cup mayonnaise
2 tsp lemon juice
grated rind of 1 lemon

NUTRITION
Calories *514*; Sugars *4 g*; Protein *9 g*;
Carbohydrate *37 g*; Fat *37 g*; Saturates *8 g*

⭐⭐⭐   moderate

🕐   25 mins

🕐   35 mins

This makes a luscious side dish to serve with meat, or serve it on its own as a satisfying vegetarian main course. Goat cheese is a traditional food of Mexico.

Potatoes *with* Goat Cheese

SERVES 4

2 lb 12 oz/1.25 kg baking potatoes, cut into chunks
pinch of salt
pinch of sugar
1 cup vegetable or chicken bouillon
3 garlic cloves, chopped finely
¾ cup homemade crème fraîche or sour cream
a few shakes of bottled chipotle salsa, or 1 dried chipotle, reconstituted, seeded, and thinly sliced
8 oz/225 g goat cheese, sliced
1½ cups grated mozzarella or Colby cheese
scant ⅔ cup grated Parmesan or romano cheese
salt

1 Put the potatoes into a pan of water with the salt and sugar. Bring to a boil and cook for about 10 minutes until they are half cooked.

2 Combine the crème fraîche with the bouillon, garlic, and chipotle salsa.

3 Arrange half the potatoes in a casserole. Pour half the crème fraîche sauce over the potatoes and cover with the goat cheese. Top with the remaining potatoes and the sauce.

4 Sprinkle with the grated mozzarella or Colby cheese, then with either the grated Parmesan or romano cheese.

5 Bake in a preheated oven, 350°F/180°C, for about 25 minutes or until the potatoes are tender and the cheese topping is lightly golden and crisped in places. Serve at once.

NUTRITION
Calories 725; Sugars 4 g; Protein 30 g;
Carbohydrate 56 g; Fat 43 g; Saturates 28 g

easy

2 mins

35 mins

This fish pâté is given a tart, fruity flavor by the cooked gooseberries, which complement the fish perfectly.

Smoked Fish *and* Potato Pâté

1 Cook the diced potatoes in a pan of boiling water for 10 minutes until tender, then drain well.

2 Place the cooked potatoes in a food processor or blender.

3 Add the skinned and flaked smoked mackerel and process for 30 seconds until fairly smooth. Alternatively, place the ingredients in a bowl and mash together with a fork.

4 Add the cooked gooseberries, lemon juice, and crème fraîche to the fish and potato mixture. Blend for another 10 seconds or mash well.

5 Stir in the capers, chopped gherkin, dill pickle, and chopped fresh dill. Season to taste with salt and pepper.

6 Transfer the fish pâté to a serving dish. Garnish with lemon wedges and serve with slices of toast or warm crusty bread, cut into chunks or slices.

SERVES 4

3²/₃ cups diced mealy potatoes,
10¹/₂ oz/300 g smoked mackerel, skinned and flaked
2³/₄ oz/75 g cooked gooseberries
2 tsp lemon juice
2 tbsp homemade crème fraîche or sour cream
1 tbsp capers
1 gherkin, chopped
1 tbsp chopped dill pickle
1 tbsp chopped fresh dill
salt and pepper
lemon wedges, to garnish
toast or warm crusty bread, to serve

NUTRITION
Calories *418*; Sugars *4 g*; Protein *18 g*;
Carbohydrate *32 g*; Fat *25 g*; Saturates *6 g*

⚅ easy

🕐 20 mins

🕐 10 mins

🧑‍🍳 **COOK'S TIP**

Use stewed, canned, or bottled cooked gooseberries for convenience and to save time, or when fresh gooseberries are out of season.

These fishcakes make a satisfying and quick midweek supper. The tomato sauce is flavored with a tempting combination of lemon, garlic and basil.

Tuna Fishcakes

SERVES 4

8 oz/225 g potatoes, cubed
1 tbsp olive oil
1 large shallot, chopped finely
1 garlic clove, chopped finely
1 tsp thyme leaves
14 oz/400 g canned tuna in olive oil, drained
grated rind of ½ lemon
1 tbsp chopped fresh parsley
2–3 tbsp all-purpose flour
1 egg, beaten lightly
4 oz/115 g fresh bread crumbs
½ cup vegetable oil, for pan-frying
salt and pepper
mixed salad greens, to serve

quick tomato sauce

2 tbsp olive oil
14 oz/400 g canned chopped tomatoes
1 garlic clove, crushed
1 tsp sugar
grated rind of 1 lemon
1 tbsp chopped fresh basil

NUTRITION

Calories *638*; Sugars *5 g*; Protein *35 g*;
Carbohydrate *38 g*; Fat *40 g*; Saturates *5 g*

⊛⊛⊛   moderate

🕐   35 mins

🕐   1 hr 10 mins

1 To make the tuna fishcakes, cook the potatoes in boiling salted water for 12–15 minutes until tender. Mash, leaving a few lumps, and set aside.

2 Heat the olive oil in a small skillet over low heat. Add the shallot and cook gently for 5 minutes until softened. Add the garlic and thyme leaves and cook for another 1 minute. Let cool slightly, then add to the potatoes with the tuna, lemon rind, parsley, and salt and pepper to taste. Mix well, but leave some texture.

3 Form the mixture into 6–8 cakes. Dip the cakes first in the flour, then the egg, and finally the bread crumbs to coat. Let chill for 30 minutes.

4 Meanwhile, make the tomato sauce. Put all the ingredients into a pan and bring to a boil. Cover and let simmer gently for 30 minutes. Uncover and let simmer for another 15 minutes until thickened.

5 Heat enough oil in a skillet to generously cover the bottom. When hot, add the chilled fishcakes, in batches, and cook for 3–4 minutes on each side until golden and crisp. Drain on paper towels while you cook the remaining fishcakes. Serve hot with the tomato sauce and mixed salad greens.

🍳 COOK'S TIP

The tuna can be replaced by cooked flaked salmon or haddock, if preferred. Omit the thyme leaves.

As well as being a simple supper dish, this would make a delicious addition to a brunch menu.

Salt Cod Hash

1 Sprinkle the salt over both sides of the cod fillet. Place in a shallow dish, cover, and let chill in the refrigerator for 48 hours. When ready to cook, remove the cod from the refrigerator and rinse under cold running water. Let soak in cold water for 2 hours, then drain well.

2 Bring a large pan of water to a boil over low heat. Add the fish, then remove from the heat and let stand for 10 minutes. Drain the fish on paper towels and flake the flesh. Set aside. Discard the cooking water.

3 Bring a pan of water to a boil over medium heat. Add the eggs and let simmer for 7–9 minutes from when the water returns to a boil—7 minutes for a slightly soft center, 9 for a firm center. Drain, then plunge the eggs into cold water. Shell the eggs and coarsely chop. Set aside.

4 Heat the olive oil in a large skillet over medium heat. Add the bacon and cook for 4–5 minutes until crisp and browned. Remove with a draining spoon and drain on paper towels. Put the potatoes and garlic in the pan and cook over medium heat for 8–10 minutes until crisp and golden. Meanwhile, toast the bread on both sides. Drizzle the bread with olive oil and set aside.

5 Add the plum tomatoes, bacon, fish, vinegar, and reserved chopped egg to the potatoes and garlic. Cook for 2 minutes. Stir in the parsley and season to taste with salt and pepper. Put the toast onto serving plates and top with the hash. Garnish with a few sprigs of fresh parsley. Serve.

SERVES 4

1 oz/25 g sea salt
1 lb 10 oz/750 g fresh boneless cod fillet
4 eggs
3 tbsp olive oil, plus extra for drizzling
8 bacon slices, chopped
generous 4 cups main-crop potatoes, diced
8 garlic cloves
8 thick slices good-quality white bread
2 plum tomatoes, peeled and chopped
2 tsp red wine vinegar
2 tbsp chopped fresh parsley
salt and pepper
fresh flatleaf parsley sprigs, to garnish

NUTRITION
Calories 857; Sugars 5 g; Protein 58 g; Carbohydrate 82 g; Fat 36 g; Saturates 10 g

★★★★ challenging

50 hrs 5 mins

30 mins

These small crab cakes are based on a traditional Thai recipe. They make a delicious snack when served with this sweet and sour cucumber sauce.

Thai Potato Crab Cakes

SERVES 4

2²/₃ cups diced mealy potatoes
6 oz/175 g white crab meat, drained
   if canned
4 scallions, chopped
1 tsp light soy sauce
½ tsp sesame oil
1 tsp chopped lemongrass
1 tsp lime juice
3 tbsp all-purpose flour
2 tbsp vegetable oil
salt and pepper

sauce

4 tbsp finely chopped cucumber
2 tbsp honey
1 tbsp garlic wine vinegar
½ tsp light soy sauce
1 chopped fresh red chile

to garnish

1 fresh red chile sliced
cucumber slices

NUTRITION

Calories *254*; Sugars *9 g*; Protein *12 g*;
Carbohydrate *40 g*; Fat *6 g*; Saturates *1 g*

easy
10 mins
30 mins

1 Cook the diced potatoes in a pan of boiling water for 10 minutes until cooked through. Drain well and mash.

2 Mix the crab meat into the potato with the scallions, soy sauce, sesame oil, lemongrass, lime juice, and flour. Season to taste with salt and pepper.

3 Using floured hands, divide the potato mixture equally into 8 portions and form them into small rounds.

4 Heat the vegetable oil in a preheated wok or skillet over medium heat. Add the cakes, 4 at a time, and cook for 5–7 minutes, turning once. Keep warm. Repeat with the remaining cakes.

5 Meanwhile, make the sauce. Mix the chopped cucumber, honey, vinegar, soy sauce, and chopped red chile in a small serving bowl.

6 Transfer the crab cakes to a large serving plate and garnish with the sliced red chile and cucumber slices. Serve with the sauce.

These crisp little vegetable and shrimp cakes make an ideal light lunch or supper, accompanied by a salad.

Shrimp Rösti

1 To make the salsa, mix the tomatoes, mango, chile, red onion, cilantro, chives, olive oil, lemon juice, and seasoning together. Set aside.

2 Using a food processor or the fine blade of a box grater, finely grate the potatoes, celery root, carrot, and onion. Mix together with the shrimp, flour, and egg. Season well with salt and pepper and set aside.

3 Divide the shrimp mixture equally into 8 portions. Press each into a greased 4-inch/10-cm cutter (if you have only 1 cutter, shape the rösti individually).

4 Heat a shallow layer of vegetable oil in a large skillet over medium heat. When hot, transfer the vegetable cakes, still in the cutters, to the skillet, in 4 batches, if necessary. When the oil sizzles underneath, remove the cutters. Cook gently, pressing down with a palette knife, for 6–8 minutes on each side, until browned and the vegetables are tender. Drain on paper towels and keep warm. Serve hot with the tomato salsa and mixed salad greens.

SERVES 4

12 oz/350 g potatoes
12 oz/350 g celery root
1 carrot
1 small onion
8 oz/225 g cooked shelled shrimp, thawed if frozen and well-drained on paper towels
1/4 cup all-purpose flour
1 egg, beaten lightly
3–4 tbsp vegetable oil, for frying
salt and pepper
mixed salad greens, to serve

cherry tomato salsa
8 oz/225 g mixed cherry tomatoes such as baby plum, yellow and orange, cut into fourths
1 small mango, diced finely
1 red chile, seeded and chopped finely
1 small red onion, chopped finely
1 tbsp chopped fresh cilantro
1 tbsp chopped fresh chives
2 tbsp olive oil
2 tsp lemon juice

NUTRITION
Calories *445*; Sugars *9 g*; Protein *19 g*; Carbohydrate *29 g*; Fat *29 g*; Saturates *4 g*

✪✪✪   moderate
            10 mins
            1 hr

You need mealy, main-crop potatoes to make these fritters. Any white fish of your choice may be used.

Spicy Fish *and* Potato Fritters

SERVES 4

1 lb 2 oz/500 g potatoes, peeled and cut into even-size pieces
1 lb 2 oz/500 g white fish fillets, such as cod or haddock, skinned and boned
6 scallions, sliced
1 fresh green chile, seeded
2 garlic cloves, peeled
1 tsp salt
1 tbsp medium or hot curry paste
2 eggs, beaten
1½ cups fresh white bread crumbs
½ cup vegetable oil, for pan-frying
mango chutney, to serve (optional)

to garnish
fresh cilantro sprigs
lime wedges

NUTRITION
Calories *349*; Sugars *4 g*; Protein *31 g*;
Carbohydrate *41 g*; Fat *8 g*; Saturates *1 g*

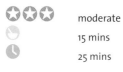

moderate
15 mins
25 mins

1 Cook the potatoes in a pan of lightly salted boiling water until tender. Drain well, then return the potatoes to the pan and place over medium heat for a few moments to dry off. Let cool slightly, then place in a food processor with the fish, scallions, chile, garlic, salt, and curry paste. Process until chopped finely and blended.

2 Transfer the potato mixture to a bowl and mix in 2 tablespoons of beaten egg and ½ cup of the bread crumbs. Place the remaining beaten egg and bread crumbs in separate dishes.

3 Divide the potato mixture equally into 8 portions and, using a spoon to help you (the mixture is quite soft), first dip each potato portion in the beaten egg and then coat it in the bread crumbs. When each portion is evenly coated, carefully shape it into an oval.

4 Heat enough vegetable oil for pan-frying in a large skillet over medium heat. When hot, add the fritters and cook for 3–4 minutes, turning frequently, until golden-brown and cooked through.

5 Drain on paper towels and garnish with lime wedges and fresh cilantro sprigs. Serve the fritters hot with mango chutney, if wished.

These fritters are delicious served with salad greens, a fresh vegetable salsa, or a chile sauce dip.

Chicken *and* Herb Fritters

1 Blend the potato, chicken, ham, herbs, and one of the eggs in a large bowl, then season well with salt and pepper.

2 Form the mixture into small balls or flat pancakes.

3 Add a little milk to the second egg and mix together.

4 Place the bread crumbs on a plate. Dip the balls in the egg and milk mixture, then roll in the bread crumbs to coat them completely.

5 Heat the vegetable oil in a large skillet over medium heat. Add the fritters and cook, turning once, until they are golden-brown on both sides. Garnish with a few sprigs of fresh parsley and serve at once with fresh salad greens.

SERVES 4

2 cups mashed potato, with butter added
1⅓ cups chopped cooked chicken
⅔ cups cooked ham, chopped finely
1 tbsp mixed herbs
2 eggs, beaten lightly
1 tbsp milk
fresh brown bread crumbs, for coating
½ cup vegetable oil, for pan-frying
salt and pepper
fresh parsley sprigs, to garnish
salad greens, to serve

NUTRITION
Calories *33*; Sugars *1 g*; Protein *16 g*;
Carbohydrate *17 g*; Fat *23 g*; Saturates *5 g*

✪✪✪   moderate

🕐   5 mins

🕐   10–15 mins

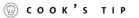 **COOK'S TIP**

A mixture of chopped fresh tarragon and parsley makes a flavorsome addition to these tasty fritters.

Serve these with bread to mop up the sauce, or make half as much mixture again, and roll into larger balls. Serve with freshly cooked rice and vegetables.

Meatballs *in* Spicy Sauce

SERVES 4

1½ cups diced mealy potatoes
8 oz/225 g ground beef or lamb
1 onion, chopped finely
1 tbsp chopped fresh cilantro
1 celery stalk, chopped finely
2 garlic cloves, crushed
2 tbsp butter
1 tbsp vegetable oil
salt and pepper
chopped fresh cilantro, to garnish

sauce

1 tbsp vegetable oil
1 onion, chopped finely
2 tsp soft brown sugar
14 oz/400 g canned chopped tomatoes
1 fresh green chile, chopped
1 tsp paprika
⅔ cup vegetable bouillon
2 tsp cornstarch

NUTRITION

Calories *95*; Sugars *2.7 g*; Protein *4.5 g*;
Carbohydrate *6.6 g*; Fat *5.8 g*; Saturates *2.3 g*

⭐⭐ easy
🕐 5 mins
🕐 1 hr 10 mins

1 Cook the diced potatoes in a pan of boiling water for 25 minutes until cooked through. Drain and transfer to a mixing bowl. Mash until smooth.

2 Add the ground beef or lamb, onion, cilantro, celery, and garlic and mix together well.

3 Bring the mixture together with your hands and roll it into 20 small balls.

4 To make the sauce, heat the vegetable oil in a pan over low heat. Add the onion and sauté for 5 minutes. Add the remaining sauce ingredients and bring to a boil, stirring. Reduce the heat and let simmer for 20 minutes.

5 Meanwhile, heat the butter and vegetable oil for the meatballs in a skillet. Add the meatballs, in batches, and cook for 10–15 minutes until browned, turning frequently. Keep warm while cooking the remainder. Serve the meatballs in a warmed shallow ovenproof dish with the sauce poured around them and garnished with cilantro.

🍳 **COOK'S TIP**

Make the potato and meatballs in advance and chill or freeze them for later use. Make sure you thaw them thoroughly before cooking.

These croquettes may be served plain as an accompaniment, or with freshly cooked vegetables or salami and a cheese sauce as an appetizer.

Croquettes *with* Ham

1 Place the potatoes in a pan with the milk and bring to a boil. Reduce to a simmer until the liquid has been absorbed and the potatoes are cooked.

2 Add the butter and mash the potatoes. Stir in the scallions, cheese, ham, celery, egg, and flour. Season to taste with salt and pepper and let cool.

3 To make the coating, whisk the eggs in a bowl. Put the bread crumbs in a separate bowl.

4 Form the potato mixture into 8 balls. First dip them in the egg, then in the whole-wheat bread crumbs.

5 To make the sauce, melt the butter in a small pan over low heat. Add the flour and cook for 1 minute. Remove from the heat and stir in the milk, bouillon, cheese, mustard, and cilantro. Bring to a boil, stirring until thickened. Reduce the heat and keep the sauce warm, stirring occasionally.

6 Heat the oil in a deep-fryer to 350°–375°F/180°–190°C, and fry the croquettes, in batches, for 5 minutes until golden. Drain well and serve with the sauce.

SERVES 4

2½ cups diced mealy potatoes
1½ cups milk
2 tbsp butter
4 scallions, chopped
¾ cup grated Colby cheese
¾ cup chopped smoked ham
1 celery stalk, diced
1 egg, beaten
½ cup all-purpose flour
2 cups vegetable oil, for deep-frying
salt and pepper

coating
2 eggs, beaten
1 cup fresh whole-wheat bread crumbs

sauce
2 tbsp butter
¼ cup all-purpose flour
⅔ cup milk
⅔ cup vegetable bouillon
¾ cup grated Colby cheese
1 tsp Dijon mustard
1 tbsp chopped fresh cilantro

NUTRITION
Calories *792*; Sugars *8 g*; Protein *28 g*;
Carbohydrate *53 g*; Fat *54 g*; Saturates *21 g*

⊛⊛⊛ moderate
  5 mins
  30 mins

This is an old Irish recipe, usually served with bacon, but it is equally delicious with a vegetarian entrée.

Colcannon

SERVES 4

8 oz/225 g green cabbage, shredded
5 tbsp milk
1½ cups diced mealy potatoes
1 large leek, chopped
pinch of freshly grated nutmeg
1 tbsp butter, melted
salt and pepper

1 Cook the shredded cabbage in a large pan of boiling salted water for about 7–10 minutes. Drain thoroughly and set aside.

2 Meanwhile, bring the milk to a boil in a separate pan, and add the potatoes and leek. Reduce the heat and let simmer for 15–20 minutes or until the potatoes and leek are cooked through.

3 Stir in the nutmeg and mash the potatoes and leek together.

4 Add the drained cabbage to the mashed potato and leek mixture and mix. Season to taste with salt and pepper.

5 Spoon the mixture into a warmed serving dish, making a hollow in the center with the back of a spoon.

6 Pour the melted butter into the hollow and serve immediately.

NUTRITION
Calories *102*; Sugars *4 g*; Protein *4 g*; Carbohydrate *14 g*; Fat *4 g*; Saturates *2 g*

easy

20 mins

20 mins

🍳 **COOK'S TIP**

There are many different varieties of cabbage, which produce hearts at varying times of the year, so you can be sure of being able to make this delicious cabbage dish all year round.

Fried potatoes are a classic favorite; here they are given extra flavor by cooking them in butter with onion, garlic, and fresh herbs.

Fried Potatoes *with* Onions

1 Cook the cubed potatoes in a pan of boiling water for 10 minutes. Drain them thoroughly.

2 Melt the butter in a large, heavy-based skillet over low heat. Add the red onion wedges, garlic, and lemon juice and cook for 2–3 minutes, stirring.

3 Add the potatoes to the pan and mix well to coat in the butter mixture.

4 Reduce the heat, then cover the skillet and cook for 25–30 minutes or until the potatoes are golden and tender.

5 Sprinkle the chopped thyme over the top of the potatoes and season to taste with salt and pepper.

6 Garnish with a few sprigs of fresh thyme, if wished, then serve immediately as a side dish to accompany broiled meats or fish.

SERVES 4

2 lb/900 g waxy potatoes, cubed
½ cup butter
1 red onion, cut into 8 pieces
2 garlic cloves, crushed
1 tsp lemon juice
2 tbsp chopped fresh thyme
salt and pepper
fresh thyme sprigs, to garnish (optional)

NUTRITION
Calories *140*; Sugars *1.2 g*; Protein *1.8 g*; Carbohydrate *14 g*; Fat *8.8 g*; Saturates *5.7 g*

⭐ very easy

🕐 5 mins

🕐 40 mins

🍽 **COOK'S TIP**

The beautifully colored purple-red onions used here have a mild, slightly sweet flavor as well as looking extremely attractive. Because of their mild taste, they are equally good eaten raw in salads .

Indian cooking has many variations of spicy potatoes. In this recipe, spinach is added for both color and flavor.

Spicy Indian Potatoes

SERVES 4

½ tsp coriander seeds
1 tsp cumin seeds
4 tbsp vegetable oil
2 cardamom pods
1 tsp grated fresh gingerroot
1 fresh red chile, chopped
1 onion, chopped
2 garlic cloves, crushed
1 lb/450 g new potatoes, cut into fourths
⅔ cup vegetable bouillon
1 lb 8 oz/675 g fresh spinach, chopped
4 tbsp plain unsweetened yogurt
salt

1 Grind the coriander and cumin seeds, using a pestle and mortar.

2 Heat the vegetable oil in a skillet over medium–low heat. Add the ground coriander and cumin seeds to the pan with the cardamom pods and ginger and cook for about 2 minutes.

3 Add the chopped chile, onion, and garlic to the pan. Cook for another 2 minutes, stirring frequently.

4 Add the potatoes to the pan together with the vegetable bouillon. Cook gently for 30 minutes or until the potatoes are cooked through.

5 Add the spinach to the pan and cook for another 5 minutes.

6 Remove the pan from the heat and stir in the yogurt. Season to taste with salt and pepper. Transfer to a serving dish and serve.

NUTRITION
Calories 65; Sugars 1.9 g; Protein 2.5 g;
Carbohydrate 6.5 g; Fat 3.4 g; Saturates 0.4 g

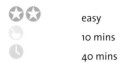

easy

10 mins

40 mins

COOK'S TIP

Use frozen spinach instead of fresh spinach, if you prefer. Thaw spinach and drain thoroughly before adding it to the dish, otherwise it will turn soggy.

This is a rich recipe which is best served with plain dark meats, such as beef or game, to complement the flavor.

Potatoes *in* Red Wine

1 Melt the butter in a heavy-based skillet over medium heat. Add the halved potatoes and cook gently for about 5 minutes, stirring constantly.

2 Add the red wine, beef bouillon, and halved shallots. Season to taste with salt and pepper and then let simmer for 30 minutes.

3 Stir in the mushrooms and herbs and cook for another 5 minutes.

4 Turn the potatoes and mushrooms into a warmed serving dish. Garnish with fresh sage leaves or cilantro sprigs and serve at once.

SERVES 4

½ cup butter
1 lb/450 g new potatoes, halved
¾ cup red wine
6 tbsp beef bouillon
8 shallots, halved
4½ oz/125 g oyster mushrooms
1 tbsp chopped fresh sage or cilantro
salt and pepper
fresh sage leaves or fresh cilantro sprigs, to garnish

NUTRITION

Calories 116; Sugars 1.4 g; Protein 1.5 g; Carbohydrate 7 g; Fat 8.7 g; Saturates 5.7 g

✪✪✪   moderate

🖐   5 mins

🕐   45 mins

COOK'S TIP

If oyster mushrooms are unavailable, other mushrooms, such as large open-cup mushrooms, can be used instead.

This is a simple, spicy dish, which is ideal with a plain main course. The nuts and celery add extra crunch.

Gingered Potatoes

SERVES 4

1 lb 8 oz/675 g waxy potatoes, cubed
2 tbsp vegetable oil
4 tsp grated fresh gingerroot
1 fresh green chile, chopped
1 celery stalk, chopped
¼ cup cashew nuts
a few strands of saffron
3 tbsp boiling water
5 tbsp butter
celery leaves, to garnish

1 Cook the potatoes in a pan of boiling water for 10 minutes, then drain.

2 Heat the vegetable oil in a heavy-based skillet over medium heat. Add the potatoes and cook, stirring constantly, for 3–4 minutes.

3 Add the grated ginger, chile, celery, and cashew nuts and cook for 1 minute.

4 Meanwhile, place the saffron strands in a small bowl. Add the boiling water and let soak for 5 minutes.

5 Add the butter, then reduce the heat and stir in the saffron mixture. Cook over a low heat for 10 minutes or until the potatoes are tender.

6 Transfer to a warmed serving dish. Garnish the gingered potatoes with the celery leaves and serve at once.

NUTRITION
Calories 325; Sugars 1 g; Protein 5 g;
Carbohydrate 30 g; Fat 21 g; Saturates 9 g

easy

20 mins

30 mins

🍳 **COOK'S TIP**

Use a nonstick, heavy-based skillet as the potato mixture is fairly dry and may stick to an ordinary pan.

In this sweet and sour dish, tender vegetables are simply stir-fried with spices and coconut milk, and flavored with lime.

Thai Potato Stir-Fry

1 Using a sharp knife, cut the potatoes into small dice.

2 Cook the diced potatoes in a large pan of boiling water for 5 minutes, then drain thoroughly.

3 Heat the vegetable oil in a preheated wok or large skillet, swirling the oil around the bottom of the wok until it is really hot.

4 Add the potatoes, diced bell peppers, carrot, zucchini, garlic, and chile to the wok, and stir-fry the vegetables for 2–3 minutes.

5 Stir in the scallions, coconut milk, chopped lemongrass, and lime juice, and stir-fry the mixture for another 5 minutes.

6 Add the lime rind and cilantro and stir-fry for 1 minute. Serve hot.

SERVES 4

2 lb/900 g waxy potatoes
2 tbsp vegetable oil
1 yellow bell pepper, seeded and diced
1 red bell pepper, seeded and diced
1 carrot, cut into thin strips
1 zucchini, cut into thin strips
2 garlic cloves, crushed
1 fresh red chile, sliced
1 bunch of scallions, halved lengthwise
½ cup coconut milk
1 tsp chopped lemongrass
2 tsp lime juice
finely grated rind of 1 lime
1 tbsp chopped fresh cilantro

NUTRITION
Calories 138; Sugars 5 g; Protein 2 g; Carbohydrate 20 g; Fat 6 g; Saturates 1 g

⊗⊗   easy
◔   10 mins
◕   20 mins

🎩 COOK'S TIP

Make sure that the potatoes are not overcooked at Step 2, otherwise the potato pieces will disintegrate when they are stir-fried in the wok.

This recipe takes a while to prepare, but it is well worth the effort. The golden potato slices coated in bread crumbs and cheese are delicious.

Cheese *and* Potato Slices

SERVES 4

2 lb/900 g large waxy potatoes, unpeeled and thickly sliced
1 cup fresh white bread crumbs
½ cup freshly grated Parmesan cheese
1½ tsp chili powder
2 eggs, beaten
2 cups vegetable oil, for deep-frying
chili powder, for dusting (optional)

1 Cook the sliced potatoes in a pan of boiling water for about 10–15 minutes or until the potatoes are just tender. Drain thoroughly.

2 Mix the bread crumbs, cheese, and chili together in a bowl, then transfer to a shallow dish. Pour the beaten eggs into a separate shallow dish.

3 First dip the potato slices in egg and then roll them in the bread crumbs to coat completely.

4 Heat the vegetable oil in a large pan to 350°F/180°C, or until a cube of bread browns in 30 seconds. Add the cheese and potato slices, in several batches, and cook for 4–5 minutes or until a golden-brown color.

5 Remove the cooked cheese and potato slices with a draining spoon and drain thoroughly on paper towels. Keep the cheese and potato slices warm while you cook the remaining batches.

6 Transfer the cheese and potato slices to warmed individual serving plates. Dust lightly with chili powder (if using) and serve immediately.

NUTRITION
Calories *560*; Sugars *3 g*; Protein *19 g*;
Carbohydrate *55 g*; Fat *31 g*; Saturates *7 g*

easy

10 mins

40 mins

🍳 COOK'S TIP

The cheese and potato slices may be coated in the bread crumb mixture in advance and then stored in the refrigerator until ready to use.

This dish is ideal with broiled or barbecued foods, as the potatoes themselves may be cooked by either method.

Broiled Potatoes *with* Lime

1 Cut the potatoes into ½-inch/1-cm thick slices.

2 Cook the potatoes in a pan of boiling water for 5–7 minutes—they should still be quite firm. Remove with a draining spoon and drain thoroughly.

3 Line a broiler pan with foil, then place the potato slices on top of the foil.

4 Brush the potatoes with the melted butter and sprinkle the chopped thyme on top. Season to taste with salt and pepper.

5 Cook the potatoes under a preheated medium–hot broiler for 10 minutes, turning them over once.

6 Meanwhile, make the lime mayonnaise. Mix the mayonnaise, lime juice, lime rind, garlic, paprika, and salt and pepper to taste together in a bowl.

7 Dust the potato slices with paprika and serve with the lime mayonnaise.

SERVES 4

1 lb/450 g potatoes, unpeeled and scrubbed
3 tbsp butter, melted
2 tbsp chopped fresh thyme
paprika, for dusting
salt and pepper

lime mayonnaise

⅔ cup mayonnaise
2 tsp lime juice
finely grated rind of 1 lime
1 garlic clove, crushed
pinch of paprika

NUTRITION

Calories 253; Sugars 0.7 g; Protein 1.8 g; Carbohydrate 12 g; Fat 22 g; Saturates 5.8 g

⭐⭐ easy

🕐 10 mins

🕐 15–20 mins

🧑‍🍳 COOK'S TIP

For an impressive side dish, thread the potato slices onto skewers and cook over a medium-hot barbecue grill.

These home-made fries are flavored with spices and cooked in the oven. Serve with Lime Mayonnaise (see page 91).

Spicy Potato Fries

SERVES 4

4 large waxy potatoes
2 sweet potatoes
4 tbsp butter, melted
½ tsp chili powder
1 tsp garam masala
salt

1 Cut the potatoes and sweet potatoes into slices about ½-inch/1-cm thick, then cut them into fries.

2 Place the cut potatoes in a large bowl of cold salted water. Let them soak for 20 minutes.

3 Remove the potato slices with a draining spoon and drain thoroughly. Pat with paper towels until completely dry.

4 Pour the melted butter onto a cookie sheet. Transfer the potato slices to the cookie sheet and spread out evenly.

5 Sprinkle with the chili powder and garam masala, turning the potato slices to coat them with the mixture.

6 Cook the fries in a preheated oven, 400°F/200°C, turning frequently, for about 40 minutes until they are browned and cooked through.

7 Drain the fries on paper towels and serve at once.

NUTRITION

Calories *328*; Sugars *2 g*; Protein *5 g*; Carbohydrate *56 g*; Fat *11 g*; Saturates *7 g*

easy

35 mins

40 mins

🍳 COOK'S TIP

Rinsing the potatoes in cold water before cooking removes the starch, thus preventing them from sticking together. Soaking the potatoes in a bowl of cold salted water actually makes the cooked fries crisper.

Small new potatoes are scrubbed and boiled in their skins, then coated in a chili mixture and roasted to perfection in the oven.

Chili Roast Potatoes

1 Cook the potatoes in a pan of boiling water for 10 minutes, then drain.

2 Pour a little of the vegetable oil into a shallow roasting pan to coat the base. Heat the oil in a preheated oven, 400°F/200°C, for 10 minutes. Add the potatoes to the pan and brush them with the hot oil.

3 Mix the chili powder, caraway seeds, and salt together in a small bowl. Sprinkle the mixture over the potatoes, turning to coat them all over.

4 Add the remaining oil to the pan and roast in the oven for about 15 minutes or until the potatoes are cooked through.

5 Using a draining spoon, remove the potatoes from the the oil, draining them well, and transfer them to a large, warmed serving dish. Sprinkle chopped basil over the top and serve at once.

SERVES 4

1 lb 2 oz/500 g small new potatoes, scrubbed
²⁄₃ cup vegetable oil
1 tsp chili powder
½ tsp caraway seeds
1 tsp salt
1 tbsp chopped fresh basil

NUTRITION
Calories *178*; Sugars *2 g*; Protein *2 g*; Carbohydrate *18 g*; Fat *11 g*; Saturates *1 g*

⊛⊛ easy

◔ 5–10 mins

🕐 30 mins

⊛ **COOK'S TIP**

Use any other spice of your choice with these roast potatoes, such as curry powder or paprika, for a variation in flavor.

This is a very simple way to jazz up roast potatoes. Serve them in the same way as roast potatoes with roasted meats or fish.

Parmesan Potatoes

SERVES 4

3 lb/1.3 kg potatoes
scant ⅔ cup freshly grated Parmesan cheese
pinch of freshly grated nutmeg
1 tbsp chopped fresh parsley
4 smoked bacon slices, cut into strips
½ cup vegetable oil, for roasting
salt

1 Cut the potatoes in half lengthwise and cook them in a pan of boiling salted water for 10 minutes. Drain them thoroughly.

2 Mix the Parmesan cheese, nutmeg, and parsley together in a shallow bowl.

3 Roll the potato pieces in the cheese mixture to coat them completely. Shake off any excess. Set aside.

4 Pour the vegetable oil into a roasting pan and heat in a preheated oven, 400°F/200°C, for 10 minutes. Remove from the oven and place the potatoes into the pan. Return to the oven and cook for 30 minutes, turning once.

5 Remove from the oven and sprinkle the bacon on top of the potatoes. Return to the oven for 15 minutes or until the potatoes and bacon are cooked. Drain off any excess fat and serve.

NUTRITION
Calories 307; Sugars 2 g; Protein 11 g;
Carbohydrate 37 g; Fat 14 g; Saturates 6 g

easy
15 mins
1 hr 5 mins

🍴 **COOK'S TIP**

If you prefer, use slices of salami or prosciutto instead of the bacon, adding it to the dish 5 minutes before the end of the cooking time.

This is a classic potato dish of layered potatoes, cream, garlic, onion, and cheese. Serve with pies, bakes, and casseroles.

Potatoes Dauphinois

1 Lightly grease a 4-cup/1-liter shallow ovenproof dish with the butter.

2 Arrange a single layer of potato slices in the base of the prepared dish.

3 Top the potato slices with half the garlic, half the sliced red onion, and one-third of the grated cheese. Season with a little salt and pepper.

4 Repeat these layers in exactly the same order, finishing with a layer of potatoes topped with the grated cheese.

5 Pour the cream over the top of the potatoes and cook in a preheated oven, 350°F/180°C, for 1½ hours or until the potatoes are cooked through and the top is browned and crispy. Serve at once, straight from the dish.

SERVES 4

1 tbsp butter
1 lb 8 oz/675 g waxy potatoes, sliced
2 garlic cloves, crushed
1 red onion, sliced
¾ cup grated Swiss cheese
1¼ cups heavy cream
salt and pepper

NUTRITION
Calories 580; Sugars 5 g; Protein 10 g;
Carbohydrate 34 g; Fat 46 g; Saturates 28 g

⭐⭐   easy

🕐   25 mins

🕐   1 hr 30 mins

👨‍🍳 **COOK'S TIP**

There are many versions of this classic potato dish, but all contain heavy cream, making it a rich and very filling side dish. This recipe must be cooked in a shallow dish to ensure there is plenty of crispy topping.

This is a potato dish which may be left to cook unattended while the remainder of the meal is being prepared, so it is ideal with casseroles.

Pommes Anna

S E R V E S   4

5 tbsp butter, melted
1 lb 8 oz/675 g waxy potatoes
4 tbsp chopped mixed fresh herbs
salt and pepper
chopped fresh herbs, to garnish

1 Brush a shallow 4-cup/1-liter ovenproof dish with a little of the butter.

2 Slice the potatoes thinly and pat dry with paper towels.

3 Arrange a layer of potato slices in the prepared dish until the base is covered. Brush with a little butter and sprinkle with one quarter of the chopped mixed herbs. Season to taste with salt and pepper.

4 Continue layering the potato slices, brushing each layer with melted butter and sprinkling with herbs, until they are all used up.

5 Brush the top layer of potato slices with butter. Cover the dish and cook in a preheated oven, 190°C/375°F, for 1½ hours.

6 Transfer to a warmed ovenproof platter and return to the oven for another 25–30 minutes until golden-brown. Garnish with chopped fresh herbs and serve at once.

N U T R I T I O N
Calories *237*; Sugars *1 g*; Protein *4 g*;
Carbohydrate *29 g*; Fat *13 g*; Saturates *8 g*

easy

15 mins

2 hrs

🍳 C O O K ' S   T I P

Make sure that the potatoes are sliced very thinly so that they are almost transparent. This will ensure that they cook thoroughly.

This potato dish is cooked in the oven with leeks and wine. It is very quick and simple to make.

Casseroled Potatoes

1 Cook the potato chunks in a pan of boiling water for 5 minutes. Drain.

2 Meanwhile, melt the butter in a skillet over low heat. Add the leeks and sauté for 5 minutes or until they have softened.

3 Spoon the partly cooked potatoes and leeks into an ovenproof dish.

4 Mix the wine, vegetable bouillon, lemon juice, and chopped mixed herbs together in a large measuring pitcher. Season to taste with salt and pepper, then pour the mixture over the potatoes.

5 Cook in a preheated oven, 375°F/190°C, for 35 minutes or until the potatoes are tender all the way through.

6 Garnish the potato casserole with lemon rind and fresh herbs (if using) and serve as an accompaniment to meat casseroles or roast meat.

SERVES 4

1 lb 8 oz/675 g waxy potatoes, cut into chunks
1 tbsp butter
2 leeks, sliced
²/₃ cup dry white wine
²/₃ cup vegetable bouillon
1 tbsp lemon juice
2 tbsp chopped mixed fresh herbs
salt and pepper

to garnish
grated lemon rind
mixed fresh herbs, optional

NUTRITION
Calories *187*; Sugars *2 g*; Protein *4 g*;
Carbohydrate *31 g*; Fat *3 g*; Saturates *2 g*

⊗⊗ easy
🕐 10 mins
🕐 50 mins

To liven up mashed potato top it with a crumble mixture flavored with herbs, mustard, and onion, which turns crunchy when it is baked.

Cheese Crumble-Topped Mash

SERVES 4

generous 5 cups diced mealy potatoes
2 tbsp butter
2 tbsp milk
½ cup grated sharp cheese or blue cheese

crumble topping

3 tbsp butter
1 onion, cut into chunks
1 garlic clove, crushed
1 tbsp whole-grain mustard
3 cups fresh whole-wheat bread crumbs
2 tbsp chopped fresh parsley
salt and pepper

1 Cook the diced potatoes in a pan of boiling water for 10 minutes or until they are cooked through.

2 Meanwhile, make the crumbly topping. Melt the butter in a skillet over low heat. Add the onion, garlic, and mustard and cook gently for 5 minutes until the onion chunks have softened, stirring constantly.

3 Put the bread crumbs into a mixing bowl and stir in the fried onion. Season to taste with salt and pepper.

4 Drain the potatoes thoroughly and place them in a mixing bowl. Add the butter and milk, then mash until smooth. Stir in the grated cheese while the mashed potato is still hot.

5 Spoon the mashed potato into a shallow ovenproof dish and sprinkle with the crumbly topping.

6 Cook in a preheated oven, 400°F/200°C, for 10–15 minutes until the crumbly topping is golden-brown and crunchy. Serve at once.

NUTRITION
Calories 131; Sugars 1.4 g; Protein 3.8 g;
Carbohydrate 17 g; Fat 5.7 g; Saturates 3.4 g

easy
10 mins
20–25 mins

🍵 **COOK'S TIP**

For extra crunch, add freshly cooked vegetables, such as celery and bell peppers, to the mashed potato at Step 4.

Hot soufflés have a reputation for being difficult to make, but this one is both simple and impressive. Make sure you serve it as soon as it is ready.

Carrot *and* Potato Soufflé

1 Brush the inside of a 3¾-cup/900-ml soufflé dish with butter. Sprinkle three-quarters of the bread crumbs over the base and sides.

2 Cut the baked potatoes in half and scoop the flesh into a mixing bowl.

3 Add the carrot, egg yolks, orange juice, and nutmeg to the potato flesh. Season to taste with salt and pepper.

4 Whisk the egg whites in a clean bowl until soft peaks form, then gently fold into the potato mixture with a metal spoon until well incorporated.

5 Gently spoon the potato and carrot mixture into the prepared soufflé dish. Sprinkle the remaining bread crumbs over the top of the mixture.

6 Cook in a preheated oven, 400°F/200°C, for 40 minutes until risen and golden. Do not open the oven door during the cooking time, otherwise the soufflé will sink. Garnish with carrot curls and serve at once.

SERVES 4

2 tbsp butter, melted
4 tbsp fresh whole-wheat bread crumbs
3 mealy potatoes, baked in their skins
2 carrots, grated
2 eggs, separated
2 tbsp orange juice
¼ tsp grated nutmeg
salt and pepper
carrot curls, to garnish

NUTRITION
Calories *294*; Sugars *6 g*; Protein *10 g*; Carbohydrate *46 g*; Fat *9 g*; Saturates *4 g*

⊗⊗   easy

🕐   15 mins

🕐   40 mins

🖐 COOK'S TIP

To bake the potatoes, prick the skins all over and cook them in a preheated oven, 375°F/190°C, for about 1 hour.

This really is a great side dish, perfect for serving with main meals cooked in the oven.

Cheese *and* Potato Pie

SERVES 4

1 lb 2 oz/500 g potatoes
1 leek, sliced
3 garlic cloves, crushed
½ cup grated Colby cheese
½ cup grated mozzarella cheese
⅓ cup freshly grated Parmesan cheese
2 tbsp chopped fresh parsley
⅔ cup light cream
⅔ cup milk
salt and pepper
chopped fresh flatleaf parsley, to garnish

1 Cook the potatoes in a pan of boiling salted water for 10 minutes. Drain well.

2 Cut the potatoes into thin slices. Arrange a layer of potatoes in the base of an ovenproof dish. Layer with a little of the leek, garlic, cheeses, and parsley. Season to taste with salt and pepper.

3 Repeat the layers until all of the ingredients have been used, finishing with a layer of cheese. Mix the cream and milk together and season to taste with salt and pepper. Pour over the potato layers.

4 Cook in a preheated oven, 325°F/160°C, for 1–1¼ hours or until the cheese is golden-brown and bubbling and the potatoes are tender.

5 Garnish with chopped fresh flatleaf parsley and serve immediately.

NUTRITION

Calories *295*; Sugars *5 g*; Protein *13 g*;
Carbohydrate *24 g*; Fat *17 g*; Saturates *11 g*

easy

15 mins

1 hr 30 mins

🍳 **COOK'S TIP**

Potatoes make a very good basis for a vegetable accompaniment and combine well with a vast range of other ingredients. They are a good source of complex carbohydrate and contain a number of vitamins.

These are ideal with a more formal meal as they take little time to prepare and look really impressive.

Mini Vegetable Puff Pastries

1 Cut the puff pastry equally into 4 pieces. Roll each piece out on a lightly floured counter to form a 5-inch/13-cm square. Place the pieces on a dampened cookie sheet and score a smaller 2.5-inch/6-cm square inside.

2 Brush with beaten egg and cook in a preheated oven, 400°F/200°C, for about 20 minutes or until risen and golden-brown.

3 While the pastry is cooking, make the filling. Cook the sweet potato in a pan of boiling water for 15 minutes, then drain well. Blanch the asparagus in a pan of boiling water for 10 minutes or until tender. Drain and set aside.

4 Remove the pastry squares from the oven. Cut out the central square of pastry and lift out. Set aside.

5 Melt the butter or margarine in a pan over low heat. Add the leek and mushrooms and sauté for 2–3 minutes. Add the lime juice, thyme, and mustard and season well with salt and pepper. Stir in the sweet potatoes and asparagus. Spoon into the pastry shells. Top with the reserved pastry squares and serve at once.

SERVES 4

pastry
1 lb/450 g puff pastry
all-purpose flour, for dusting
1 egg, beaten

filling
8 oz/225 g sweet potatoes, cubed
3½ oz/100 g baby asparagus spears
2 tbsp butter or margarine
1 leek, sliced
2 small open-cup mushrooms, sliced
1 tsp lime juice
1 tsp chopped thyme
pinch of dried mustard
salt and pepper

NUTRITION
Calories *210*; Sugars *2 g*; Protein *4 g*;
Carbohydrate *21 g*; Fat *13 g*; Saturates *1.7 g*

⊛⊛   easy
🕐   15 mins
🕐   25 mins

🍲 **COOK'S TIP**

Use a colorful selection of any vegetables you have at hand for this recipe.

Although virtually unknown in India, this dish is a very popular item on Indian restaurant menus in other parts of the world.

Bombay Potatoes

SERVES 4

2 lb 4 oz/1 kg waxy potatoes
2 tbsp ghee or vegetable oil
1 tsp panch poran spice mix
3 tsp ground turmeric
2 tbsp tomato paste
1¼ cups plain yogurt
salt
chopped fresh cilantro, to garnish

1 Put the whole potatoes into a large pan of salted cold water. Bring to a boil, then let simmer until the potatoes are just cooked, but not tender. The time depends on the size of the potato, but an average-size one should take about 15 minutes to cook.

2 Heat the ghee in a pan over medium heat. Add the panch poran, turmeric, tomato paste, yogurt, and salt and bring to a boil. Let simmer, uncovered, for 5 minutes.

3 Drain the potatoes and cut each one into 4 pieces. Add the potatoes to the pan, then cover and cook briefly. Transfer to an ovenproof casserole. Cook in a preheated oven, 350°F/180°C, for about 40 minutes or until the potatoes are tender and the sauce has thickened slightly.

4 Transfer the potatoes to a serving dish, sprinkle with chopped cilantro and serve at once.

NUTRITION

Calories 307; Sugars 9 g; Protein 9 g; Carbohydrate 51 g; Fat 9 g; Saturates 5 g

⭐ very easy
🕐 5 mins
🕐 1 hr 10 mins

🍳 COOK'S TIP

Panch poran spice mix can be bought from Asian or Indian grocery stores, or make your own from equal quantities of cumin seeds, fennel seeds, mustard seeds, nigella seeds, and fenugreek seeds.

In this classic French recipe, sliced potatoes are cooked with onions to make a delicious accompaniment to a main meal.

Potatoes Lyonnaise

1 Slice the potatoes into 5-mm/¼-inch slices. Cook in a large pan of lightly salted boiling water for about 10–12 minutes until just tender. Avoid boiling too rapidly or the potatoes will break up and lose their shape. When cooked, drain thoroughly.

2 While the potatoes are cooking, heat the oil and butter in a very large skillet. Add the onions and garlic (if using) and fry over medium heat, stirring frequently, until the onions are softened.

3 Add the cooked potato slices to the skillet and cook them with the onions and garlic, stirring occasionally, for about 5–8 minutes until the potatoes are well browned.

4 Season to taste with salt and pepper. Sprinkle over the chopped parsley to serve. If wished, transfer the potatoes and onions to a large ovenproof dish and keep warm in a slow oven until ready to serve.

SERVES 4

2 lb 12 oz/1.25 kg potatoes
4 tbsp olive oil
2 tbsp butter
2 onions, sliced
2–3 garlic cloves, crushed (optional)
salt and pepper
chopped fresh parsley, to garnish

NUTRITION
Calories 277; Sugars 4 g; Protein 5 g; Carbohydrate 40 g; Fat 12 g; Saturates 4 g

⭐ very easy

🕐 10 mins

🕐 25 mins

🍳 **COOK'S TIP**

If the potatoes blacken slightly as they are boiling, add a spoonful of lemon juice to the cooking water.

Small new potatoes, served warm in a delicious dressing. The nutritional information is for the potato salad with the curry dressing only.

Three-Way Potato Salad

SERVES 4

1 lb 2 oz/500 g new potatoes (for each dressing)
salt and pepper
fresh herbs, to garnish

light curry dressing
1 tbsp vegetable oil
1 tbsp medium curry paste
1 small onion, chopped
1 tbsp mango chutney, chopped
6 tbsp plain yogurt
3 tbsp light cream, plus extra to garnish
2 tbsp mayonnaise

vinaigrette dressing
6 tbsp hazelnut oil
3 tbsp cider vinegar
1 tsp whole-grain mustard
1 tsp superfine sugar
few fresh basil leaves, torn

parsley cream
3 tbsp lowfat mayonnaise
⅔ cup sour cream
4 scallions, chopped finely
1 tbsp chopped fresh parsley

NUTRITION
Calories 310; Sugars 12 g; Protein 6 g;
Carbohydrate 31 g; Fat 19 g; Saturates 4 g

★ very easy
🕐 10–20 mins
🕐 20 mins

1 To make the light curry dressing, heat the vegetable oil in a pan over low heat. Add the curry paste and onion and cook, stirring frequently, until the onion has softened. Remove from the heat and let cool slightly.

2 Mix the mango chutney, yogurt, cream, and mayonnaise together. Add the curry mixture and blend together. Season to taste with salt and pepper.

3 To make the vinaigrette dressing, whisk the oil, vinegar, mustard, sugar, and basil together in a small jug or bowl. Season to taste with salt and pepper.

4 To make the parsley cream, combine the mayonnaise, sour cream, scallions, and parsley, mixing well. Season to taste with salt and pepper.

5 Cook the potatoes in lightly salted boiling water until just tender. Drain well and let cool for 5 minutes, then add the chosen dressing, tossing to coat. Serve, garnished with fresh herbs, spooning a little light cream onto the potatoes if you have used the curry dressing.

These earthy potatoes are delicious either as a side dish with simmered or braised meat, or as a vegetarian main course.

Potatoes *in* Green Sauce

1 Put the potatoes in a pan of salted water. Bring to a boil and cook for about 15 minutes or until almost tender. Do not overcook them. Drain the potatoes and set aside.

2 Meanwhile, lightly char the onion, garlic, chile, and tomatillos or tomatoes in a heavy-based, ungreased skillet. Let cool, and when cool enough to handle, peel and chop the onion, garlic, and chile; chop the tomatillos or tomatoes. Put into a food processor or blender with half the bouillon and process to form a purée. Add the cumin, thyme, and oregano.

3 Heat the vegetable oil in the heavy-based skillet over low heat. Add the purée and cook for 5 minutes, stirring, to reduce and concentrate the flavors.

4 Add the potatoes and zucchini to the purée and pour in the rest of the bouillon. Add about half the cilantro and cook for another 5 minutes or until the zucchini are tender.

5 Transfer to a serving bowl and serve sprinkled with the remaining chopped cilantro to garnish.

SERVES 4

2 lb 4 oz/1 kg small waxy potatoes
1 onion, halved and unpeeled
8 garlic cloves, unpeeled
1 fresh green chile
8 tomatillos, outer husks removed, or small tart tomatoes
scant 1 cup chicken, meat, or vegetable bouillon, preferably home-made
½ tsp ground cumin
1 fresh thyme sprig or good pinch of dried thyme
1 fresh oregano sprig or good pinch of dried oregano
2 tbsp vegetable or extra virgin olive oil
1 zucchini, chopped coarsely
1 bunch of fresh cilantro, chopped
salt

NUTRITION
Calories *61*; Sugars *1.4 g*; Protein *2 g*; Carbohydrate *11 g*; Fat *1.4 g*; Saturates *0.2 g*

⭐⭐   easy
🕐   5 mins
🕐   25 mins

👨‍🍳 **COOK'S TIP**

If fresh cilantro is unavailable, replace with flatleaf parsley.

Serve these as an accompaniment to other barbecue grill dishes or with a spicy dip as an appetizer while the main dishes are being cooked.

Spicy Sweet Potato Slices

SERVES 4

1 lb/450 g sweet potatoes, unpeeled
2 tbsp corn oil
1 tsp chili sauce
salt and pepper

1 Bring a large pan of water to a boil over medium heat. Add the sweet potatoes and parboil them for 10 minutes. Drain thoroughly and transfer to a cutting board.

2 Peel the potatoes and cut them into thick slices.

3 To make the coating for the potatoes, mix together the corn oil, chili sauce, and salt and pepper to taste in a small bowl.

4 Brush the spicy mixture liberally over one side of the potatoes. Transfer the potatoes to a lit barbecue, oil side down, and cook over medium–hot coals for 5–6 minutes.

5 Lightly brush the tops of the potatoes with the oil, then turn them over and cook for another 5 minutes or until crisp and golden.

6 Transfer the potatoes to a warmed serving dish and serve at once.

NUTRITION
Calories *178*; Sugars *1 g*; Protein *2 g*;
Carbohydrate *32 g*; Fat *6 g*; Saturates *0.7 g*

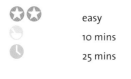

easy

10 mins

25 mins

🍴 **COOK'S TIP**

For a simple spicy dip, combine ⅔ cup sour cream with ½ teaspoon of sugar, ½ teaspoon of Dijon mustard, and salt and pepper to taste. Chill until required.

Serve this tasty barbecued potato dish with grilled kabobs, bean burgers, or vegetarian sausages.

Grilled Potato Wedges

1 Bring a large pan of water to a boil over medium heat. Add the potatoes and parboil them for 10 minutes. Drain the potatoes and refresh under cold running water, then drain them again thoroughly.

2 Transfer the potatoes to a cutting board. When the potatoes are cold enough to handle, cut them into thick wedges, but do not peel.

3 Heat the olive oil and butter in a small pan together with the garlic. Cook gently until the garlic begins to brown, then remove the pan from the heat.

4 Stir the herbs and salt and pepper to taste into the mixture in the pan.

5 Brush the herb mixture all over the potato wedges.

6 Transfer the potatoes to a lit barbecue and cook over hot coals for about 10–15 minutes, brushing liberally with any of the remaining herb and butter mixture, until just tender.

7 Transfer the garlic potato wedges to a warmed serving plate and serve as an appetizer or as a side dish.

SERVES 4

3 large baking potatoes, scrubbed
4 tbsp olive oil
2 tbsp butter
2 garlic cloves, chopped
1 tbsp chopped fresh rosemary
1 tbsp chopped fresh parsley
1 tbsp chopped fresh thyme
salt and pepper

COOK'S TIP

You may find it easier to grill these potatoes on a hinged rack or in a specially designed roasting pan.

NUTRITION
Calories 257; Sugars 1 g; Protein 3 g; Carbohydrate 26 g; Fat 16 g; Saturates 5 g

⭐ very easy
🕐 10 mins
🕐 30–35 mins

Vegetarian *and* Vegan Suppers

The potato has become a valued staple of the vegetarian diet, yet anyone who thought this would make for dull eating will be pleasantly surprised by the rich variety of dishes in this chapter. In addition to traditional hearty bakes and hotpots, there are also influences from around the world in dishes such as Bean Curd Stir-Fry from China, and Potato & Vegetable Curry from India. They all make exciting eating at any time of year.

This is a quick one-pan dish, which is ideal for a snack. Packed with color and flavor it is very versatile, as you can add other vegetables.

Pepper *and* Mushroom Hash

SERVES 4

1 lb 8 oz/675 g potatoes, cubed
1 tbsp olive oil
2 garlic cloves, crushed
1 green bell pepper, seeded and cubed
1 yellow bell pepper, seeded and cubed
3 tomatoes, diced
1 cup white mushrooms, halved
1 tbsp Worcestershire sauce
2 tbsp chopped fresh basil
salt and pepper
fresh basil leaves, to garnish

1 Cook the potatoes in a pan of boiling salted water for 7–8 minutes. Drain well and set aside.

2 Heat the olive oil in a large, heavy-based skillet over medium heat. Add the potatoes and cook, stirring constantly, for 8–10 minutes until browned.

3 Add the garlic and bell peppers and cook, stirring frequently, for about 2–3 minutes.

4 Stir in the tomatoes and mushrooms and cook, stirring frequently, for about 5–6 minutes.

5 Stir in the Worcestershire sauce and chopped basil and season to taste with salt and pepper. Transfer to a warmed serving dish. Garnish with basil leaves and serve.

NUTRITION
Calories *182*; Sugars *6 g*; Protein *5 g*;
Carbohydrate *34 g*; Fat *4 g*; Saturates *0.5 g*

easy

5 mins

30 mins

🍳 COOK'S TIP

Most brands of Worcestershire sauce contain anchovies, so if you are vegetarian, check the label to make sure you choose a vegetarian variety.

Very little meat is eaten in India, and the Indian diet is mainly vegetarian. This potato curry with added vegetables makes a substantial entrée.

Potato *and* Vegetable Curry

1 Heat the vegetable oil in a large heavy-based pan or skillet over low heat. Add the potato chunks, onion, and garlic and cook, stirring frequently, for about 2–3 minutes.

2 Add the garam masala, turmeric, ground cumin, ground coriander, grated ginger, and chopped chile to the pan, mixing the spices into the vegetables. Cook over low heat, stirring constantly, for 1 minute.

3 Add the cauliflower florets, tomatoes, peas, chopped cilantro, and vegetable bouillon to the curry mixture.

4 Cook the potato curry over low heat for 30–40 minutes or until the potatoes are tender and completely cooked through.

5 Garnish the potato curry with fresh cilantro and serve with plain boiled rice or warm Indian bread.

SERVES 4

4 tbsp vegetable oil
1 lb 8 oz/675 g waxy potatoes, cut into large chunks
2 onions, cut into fourths
3 garlic cloves, crushed
1 tsp garam masala
½ tsp turmeric
½ tsp ground cumin
½ tsp ground coriander
2 tsp grated fresh gingerroot
1 fresh red chile, chopped
8 oz/225 g cauliflower florets
4 tomatoes, peeled and cut into fourths
¾ cup frozen peas
2 tbsp chopped fresh cilantro
1¼ cups vegetable bouillon
shredded fresh cilantro, to garnish
boiled rice or warm Indian bread to serve

NUTRITION
Calories *301*; Sugars *10 g*; Protein *9 g*; Carbohydrate *41 g*; Fat *12 g*; Saturates *1 g*

easy

5 mins

45 mins

COOK'S TIP

Using a large, heavy-based pan or skillet for this recipe ensures that the potatoes are cooked thoroughly.

Fried mashed potato and leftover greens is best known as Bubble & Squeak. It is served as an accompaniment.

Bubble *and* Squeak

SERVES 4

2⅔ cups mealy diced potatoes
8 oz/225 g Savoy cabbage, shredded
5 tbsp vegetable oil
2 leeks, chopped
1 garlic clove, crushed
8 oz/225 g smoked bean curd, drained and cubed
salt and pepper
shredded cooked leek, to garnish

1 Cook the diced potatoes in a pan of lightly salted boiling water for 10 minutes until tender. Drain and mash the potatoes.

2 Meanwhile, blanch the cabbage in a separate pan of boiling water for about 5 minutes. Drain well and add to the potato.

3 Heat the oil in a heavy-based skillet over low heat. Add the leeks and garlic and cook for 2–3 minutes. Stir into the potato and cabbage mixture.

4 Add the smoked bean curd and season well with salt and pepper. Cook over medium heat for 10 minutes.

5 Carefully turn the whole mixture over and continue to cook over medium heat for another 5–7 minutes until crispy underneath. Transfer to a large serving dish, garnish with shredded leek and serve at once.

NUTRITION
Calories *301*; Sugars *5 g*; Protein *11 g*;
Carbohydrate *24 g*; Fat *18 g*; Saturates *2 g*

easy

15 mins

40 mins

🍳 **COOK'S TIP**

This version of the classic recipe is a perfect main meal, as the smoked bean curd cubes added to the basic bubble and squeak mixture make it very substantial and nourishing.

These cakes, made from a spicy vegetable mixture, are delightfully easy to make and taste delicious.

Spicy Vegetable Cakes

1 Place the potatoes, onion, and cauliflower florets in a pan of water and bring to a boil. Reduce the heat and let simmer until the potatoes are cooked through. Remove the vegetables from the pan with a draining spoon and drain thoroughly. Set aside.

2 Add the peas and spinach purée to the vegetables and mix, mashing down thoroughly with a fork.

3 Using a sharp knife, finely chop the green chiles and cilantro leaves.

4 Mix the chiles and cilantro leaves with the ginger, garlic, ground coriander, turmeric, and salt.

5 Blend the spice mixture into the vegetables, mixing to make a paste.

6 Sprinkle the bread crumbs onto a large plate.

7 Break off 10–12 small balls from the spice paste. Flatten them with the palm of your hand to make flat, round shapes.

8 Dip each cake in the bread crumbs, coating well.

9 Heat the vegetable oil in a heavy-based skillet over medium heat. Add the cakes, in batches, and cook until golden-brown, turning occasionally. Transfer to serving plates and garnish with fresh chile strips and a few sprigs of fresh cilantro. Serve hot.

MAKES 12

3½ cups potatoes, sliced
1 onion, sliced
½ medium cauliflower, cut into small florets
scant ½ cup peas
1 tbsp spinach purée
2–3 fresh green chiles
1 tbsp fresh cilantro leaves
1 tsp finely chopped fresh gingerroot
1 tsp crushed garlic
1 tsp ground coriander
pinch of turmeric
1 tsp salt
1 cup bread crumbs
1¼ cups vegetable oil

garnish
fresh chile strips
fresh cilantro sprigs

NUTRITION
Calories *268*; Sugars *1 g*; Protein *2 g*; Carbohydrate *9 g*; Fat *25 g*; Saturates *3 g*

easy
20 mins
25 mins

This curry is very popular in India. There are many different ways of cooking garbanzo beans, but this spicy version is probably one of the most delicious.

Garbanzo Bean Curry

SERVES 4

6 tbsp vegetable oil
2 onions, sliced
1 tsp finely chopped fresh gingerroot
1 tsp ground cumin
1 tsp ground coriander
1 tsp fresh garlic, crushed
1 tsp chili powder
2 fresh green chiles
1 tbsp fresh cilantro leaves
$\frac{2}{3}$ cup water
10$\frac{1}{2}$ oz/300 g potatoes
14 oz/400 g canned garbanzo beans, drained
1 tbsp lemon juice
chapatis, to serve (optional)

1 Heat the vegetable oil in a large pan over medium heat.

2 Add the onions and cook, stirring occasionally, until golden-brown.

3 Reduce the heat, then add the ginger, ground cumin, ground coriander, garlic, chili powder, fresh green chiles, and fresh cilantro leaves to the pan and cook for 2 minutes.

4 Add the water to the mixture in the pan and stir to mix.

5 Using a sharp knife, cut the potato into small dice.

6 Add the potatoes and the drained garbanzo beans to the mixture in the pan. Cover and let simmer, stirring occasionally, for 5–7 minutes.

7 Sprinkle the lemon juice over the curry.

8 Transfer the garbanzo bean curry to 4 large serving dishes. Serve the curry hot with chapatis, if you wish.

NUTRITION

Calories 114; Sugars 2 g; Protein 3 g; Carbohydrate 10 g; Fat 7 g; Saturates 0.7 g

⭐⭐⭐   moderate
🕐   5–10 mins
🕐   15 mins

👨‍🍳 COOK'S TIP

Using canned garbanzo beans saves time, but you can use dried garbanzo beans, if you prefer. Soak overnight, then boil for 15–20 minutes or until soft.

This bread can be quite rich and is usually made for special occasions. It can be eaten on its own or with a vegetable curry.

Vegetable-Stuffed Paratas

1 To make the paratas, mix the flour, salt, water, and ghee to form a dough.

2 Divide the dough equally into 6–8 portions. Roll each portion out onto a floured counter. Brush the center of the dough portions with ½ teaspoon of ghee. Fold the dough portions in half and roll into a pipelike shape, then flatten with the palms of your hands and roll around a finger to form a coil. Roll out again, using flour to dust when necessary, to form a round about 7 inches/18 cm in diameter.

3 Place the potatoes in a pan of boiling water and cook until soft. Drain thoroughly, then mash. Set aside.

4 Blend the turmeric, garam masala, ginger, cilantro leaves, chiles, and salt together in a bowl.

5 Add the spice mixture to the mashed potato and mix well. Spread about 1 tablespoon of the spicy potato mixture on each dough portion and cover with another rolled-out piece of dough. Seal the edges well.

6 Heat 2 teaspoons of ghee in a heavy-based skillet over medium heat. Place the paratas gently in the pan, in batches, and cook, turning and moving them about gently with a flat spoon, until golden.

7 Remove the paratas from the skillet and serve at once.

SERVES 4

dough
1¾ cups whole-wheat flour (ata or chapati flour), plus extra for dusting
½ tsp salt
scant 1 cup water
3½ oz/100 g ghee
2½ tbsp ghee, for frying

filling
1 lb 8 oz/675 g potatoes
½ tsp turmeric
1 tsp garam masala
1 tsp finely chopped fresh gingerroot
1 tbsp fresh cilantro leaves
3 fresh green chiles, chopped finely
1 tsp salt

NUTRITION
Calories *391*; Sugars *2 g*; Protein *6 g*;
Carbohydrate *40 g*; Fat *24 g*; Saturates *2.5 g*

✪✪✪ moderate

25 mins

30–35 mins

Pakoras are eaten all over India. They are made in many different ways and with a variety of fillings. Sometimes they are served with yogurt.

Pakoras

SERVES 4

6 tbsp gram flour
½ tsp salt
1 tsp chili powder
1 tsp baking powder
1½ tsp white cumin seeds
1 tsp pomegranate seeds
1¼ cups water
1 tbsp finely chopped fresh cilantro leaves
vegetables of your choice: cauliflower cut into small florets, onions cut into rings, sliced potatoes, sliced eggplants, or fresh spinach leaves
2 cups vegetable oil, for deep-frying
fresh cilantro sprigs, to garnish

1 Strain the gram flour into a large mixing bowl. Add the salt, chili powder, baking powder, cumin, and pomegranate seeds, and blend together well. Pour in the water and beat thoroughly to form a smooth batter.

2 Add the chopped cilantro leaves and mix. Set the batter aside.

3 Dip the prepared vegetables of your choice into the batter, carefully shaking off the excess batter.

4 Heat enough vegetable oil to cover the pakoras in a deep, heavy-based pan to 350°F/180°C, or until a cube of bread browns in 30 seconds. Place the batter-coated vegetables in the oil and deep-fry, in batches, turning once.

5 Repeat this process until all of the batter has been used up.

6 Transfer the vegetables to paper towels and drain thoroughly. Transfer to a large serving plate, garnish with a few sprigs of fresh cilantro and serve.

NUTRITION
Calories 331; Sugars 5 g; Protein 9 g;
Carbohydrate 27 g; Fat 22 g; Saturates 3 g

very easy

15 mins

15–20 mins

🏅 **COOK'S TIP**

When cooking pakoras, it is important to use oil at the correct temperature. If the oil is too hot, the outside of the food will burn, as will the spices, before the inside is cooked. If the oil is too cool, the food will be soaked with oil.

This is based on a Moroccan dish in which potatoes are spiced with cilantro and cumin and cooked in a lemon sauce.

Potato *and* Lemon Casserole

1 Heat the olive oil in a flameproof casserole over medium heat. Add the onion and sauté, stirring frequently, for 3 minutes.

2 Add the garlic and cook for 30 seconds. Stir in the spices and cook, stirring constantly, for 1 minute.

3 Add the carrot, turnips, zucchini, and potatoes, and stir to coat in the oil.

4 Add the lemon juice and rind and the vegetable bouillon. Season to taste with salt and pepper. Cover and cook over medium heat, stirring occasionally, for 20–30 minutes until tender.

5 Remove the lid, sprinkle in the cilantro and stir well. Serve at once.

SERVES 4

½ cup olive oil
2 red onions, cut into 8 pieces
3 garlic cloves, crushed
2 tsp ground cumin
2 tsp ground coriander
pinch of cayenne pepper
1 carrot, sliced thickly
2 small turnips, cut into fourths
1 zucchini, sliced
1 lb 2 oz/500 g potatoes, sliced thickly
juice and grated rind of 2 large lemons
1¼ cups vegetable bouillon
2 tbsp chopped fresh cilantro
salt and pepper

NUTRITION
Calories *338*; Sugars *8 g*; Protein *5 g*;
Carbohydrate *29 g*; Fat *23 g*; Saturates *2 g*

✪✪   easy

🕐   15 mins

🕐   35 mins

🍳 **COOK'S TIP**

Check the vegetables while they are cooking, as they may begin to stick to the pan. Add a little more boiling water or bouillon, if necessary.

This is a quick dish to prepare, making it ideal as a midweek supper dish after a busy day at work!

Bean Curd Stir-Fry

SERVES 4

1¼ cups cubed potatoes
1 tbsp vegetable oil
1 red onion, sliced
8 oz/225 g firm bean curd, drained and diced
2 zucchini, diced
8 canned artichoke hearts, halved
⅔ cup strained tomatoes
1 tbsp sweet chili sauce
1 tbsp soy sauce
1 tsp superfine sugar
2 tbsp chopped basil
salt and pepper

1 Cook the potatoes in a pan of boiling water for 10 minutes. Drain thoroughly and set aside until required.

2 Heat the vegetable oil in a preheated wok or large skillet over medium heat. Add the red onion and sauté for 2 minutes until the onion has softened, stirring constantly.

3 Stir the diced bean curd and zucchini into the softened onion and cook for 3–4 minutes until they begin to brown slightly.

4 Add the cooked potatoes to the wok or skillet, stirring to mix.

5 Stir in the artichoke hearts, strained tomatoes, sweet chili sauce, soy sauce, sugar, and basil.

6 Season to taste with salt and pepper and cook for another 5 minutes, stirring well.

7 Transfer the stir-fry to 4 serving dishes and serve at once.

NUTRITION
Calories *124*; Sugars *2 g*; Protein *6 g*;
Carbohydrate *11 g*; Fat *6 g*; Saturates *1 g*

⭐⭐⭐   moderate
🕐   5 mins
🕐   25 mins

COOK'S TIP

Canned artichoke hearts should be drained thoroughly and rinsed before use because they often have salt added.

Enticing little tasty mouthfuls of sweet potato, served hot and sizzling from the pan with a fresh tomato sauce.

Sweet Potato Cakes

1 Make the soy-tomato sauce. Heat the vegetable oil in a preheated wok over medium heat. Add the garlic and ginger and cook for about 1 minute. Add the tomatoes and cook for another 2 minutes. Remove from the heat and stir in the soy sauce, lime, and cilantro. Set aside and keep warm.

2 Peel the sweet potatoes and grate finely (you can do this quickly in a food processor). Place the garlic, chile, and fresh cilantro in a mortar and crush to a smooth paste with a pestle. Stir in the soy sauce and mix with the sweet potatoes.

3 Divide the mixture equally into 12 portions. Dip them into the flour and pat into a flat, round patty shape.

4 Heat a shallow layer of vegetable oil in a wide skillet over high heat. Add the sweet potato cakes, in batches, and cook until golden, turning once.

5 Drain on paper towels and sprinkle with sesame seeds. Transfer to a serving plate, garnish with a few sprigs of fresh herbs and serve hot with a spoonful of the soy-tomato sauce.

SERVES 4

1 lb 2 oz/500 g sweet potatoes
2 garlic cloves, crushed
1 small fresh green chile, chopped
2 fresh cilantro sprigs, chopped
1 tbsp dark soy sauce
all-purpose flour, for shaping
½ cup vegetable oil, for pan-frying
sesame seeds, for sprinkling
fresh herb sprigs, to garnish

soy-tomato sauce
2 tsp vegetable oil
1 garlic clove, finely chopped
1½ tsp finely chopped fresh gingerroot
3 tomatoes, peeled and chopped
2 tbsp dark soy sauce
1 tbsp lime juice
2 tbsp chopped fresh cilantro

NUTRITION
Calories *349*; Sugars *9 g*; Protein *4 g*;
Carbohydrate *32 g*; Fat *24 g*; Saturates *3 g*

⭐⭐ easy
🕐 10–15 mins
🕐 15 mins

Vegetable Savories

This chapter proves that meat does not have to be involved in a truly excellent main meal. In this section you will find dishes from other parts of the world, such as Potato & Spinach Gnocchi from Italy, and Potato & Eggplant Gratin, similar to Moussaka, from Greece. Family favorites such as Nutty Harvest Loaf, and Vegetable Hotpot have been included, while the needs of the dinner party have not been forgotten with the spectacular Three Cheese Soufflé. Whatever the occasion, you are sure to find something here to satisfy the heartiest of appetites.

Sweet potatoes have very dense flesh and a delicious, sweet, earthy taste, which contrasts well with the flavor of the ginger.

Sweet Potato *and* Leek Patties

SERVES 4

2 lb/900 g sweet potato
4 tsp corn oil
2 leeks, trimmed and finely chopped
1 garlic clove, crushed
2 tsp finely chopped fresh gingerroot
7 oz/200 g canned corn, drained
2 tbsp lowfat plain yogurt
generous ½ cup whole-wheat flour
salt and pepper

ginger sauce
2 tbsp white wine vinegar
2 tsp superfine sugar
1 fresh red chile, seeded and chopped
1-inch/2.5-cm piece fresh gingerroot, cut into
   thin strips
2 tbsp ginger wine
4 tbsp vegetable bouillon
1 tsp cornstarch

TO SERVE
lettuce leaves
1 scallion, shredded

NUTRITION
Calories *403*; Sugars *34 g*; Protein *8 g*;
Carbohydrate *67 g*; Fat *12 g*; Saturates *2 g*

⊛⊛⊛   moderate

🖐   45 mins

🕐   40 mins

1 Peel the potatoes. Cut into thick cubes and boil for 10–15 minutes. Drain the potatoes well and mash. Let cool.

2 Heat 2 teaspoons of corn oil in a large skillet over medium–low heat. Add the leeks, garlic, and ginger and cook for 2–3 minutes. Stir into the potato with the corn, yogurt, and seasoning. Form into 8 patties and toss in the flour. Let chill for 30 minutes. Place the patties on a broiler rack and lightly brush with corn oil. Cook under a preheated hot broiler for 5 minutes, then turn over, brush with corn oil, and broil for another 5 minutes.

3 To make the sauce, place the vinegar, sugar, chile, and ginger in a pan and let simmer for about 5 minutes. Stir in the wine. Blend the bouillon and cornstarch together and add to the sauce, stirring until thickened. Serve the patties with lettuce and scallions, and a little of the ginger sauce on the side.

🍳 COOK'S TIP

If you prefer, use babu peas instead of the corn. Cook them first if they are frozen.

Ratatouille is a classic dish of vegetables cooked in a tomato and herb sauce. Here it is topped with diced potatoes and cheese.

Vegetable Ratatouille

1 Peel and finely chop the onions and garlic. Rinse, seed, and slice the bell peppers. Rinse, trim, and cut the eggplant into small dice. Rinse, trim, and thinly slice the zucchini.

2 Place the onion, garlic and bell peppers in a large pan. Add the tomatoes, and stir in the bouquet garni, tomato paste, and salt and pepper to taste. Bring to a boil, cover, and let simmer for 10 minutes, stirring halfway through. Stir in the prepared eggplant and zucchini and cook, uncovered, for another 10 minutes, stirring occasionally.

3 Meanwhile, peel the potatoes and cut into 1-inch/2.5-cm cubes. Place the potatoes into another pan and cover with water. Bring to a boil and cook for 10–12 minutes until tender. Drain and set aside.

4 Transfer the vegetables to a heatproof gratin dish. Arrange the cooked potatoes evenly over the vegetables.

5 Sprinkle grated cheese over the potatoes and place under a preheated medium–hot broiler for 5 minutes until golden, bubbling, and hot. Serve garnished with chopped chives.

SERVES 4

2 onions
1 garlic clove
1 red bell pepper
1 green bell pepper
1 eggplant
2 zucchini
1 lb 12 oz/800 g canned chopped tomatoes
1 bouquet garni
2 tbsp tomato paste
2 lb/900 g potatoes
¾ cup grated reduced-fat sharp Colby cheese
salt and pepper
2 tbsp chopped fresh chives, to garnish

NUTRITION
Calories 287; Sugars 13 g; Protein 14 g; Carbohydrate 53 g; Fat 4 g; Saturates 2 g

✪✪✪✪ challenging
🕐 15 mins
🕐 25 mins

🍳 **COOK'S TIP**

You can vary the vegetables in this dish depending on seasonal availability and personal preference. Try broccoli, carrots, or corn, if you prefer.

Potatoes make a great pizza base and this recipe is well worth making, rather than using a store-bought base, both for texture and flavor.

Potato *and* Pepperoni Pizza

SERVES 4

1 tbsp butter, plus extra for greasing
1–2 tbsp all-purpose flour, for dusting
generous 5 cups diced mealy potatoes
2 garlic cloves, crushed
2 tbsp chopped mixed fresh herbs
1 egg, beaten
6 tbsp strained tomatoes
2 tbsp tomato paste
1¾ oz/50 g pepperoni slices
1 green bell pepper, cut into strips
1 yellow bell pepper, cut into strips
2 large open-cup mushrooms, sliced
1 oz/25 g pitted black olives, cut into fourths
4½ oz/125 g mozzarella cheese, sliced

1 Grease and flour a 9-inch/23-cm pizza pan.

2 Cook the diced potatoes in a pan of boiling water for 10 minutes or until cooked through. Drain and mash until smooth. Transfer the mashed potato to a mixing bowl and stir in the butter, garlic, herbs, and egg.

3 Spread the mixture into the prepared pizza pan. Cook in a preheated oven, 425°F/220°C, for 7–10 minutes or until the pizza base begins to set.

4 Mix the strained tomatoes and tomato paste together and spoon this over the pizza base, to within ½ inch/1 cm of the edge of the base.

5 Arrange the pepperoni, bell peppers, mushrooms, and olives evenly on top of the strained tomatoes.

6 Sprinkle the mozzarella cheese on top of the pizza. Return to the oven for 20 minutes or until the base is cooked through and the cheese has melted.

NUTRITION
Calories 234; Sugars 5 g; Protein 4 g;
Carbohydrate 30 g; Fat 12 g; Saturates 1 g

✪✪✪ moderate
🕐 20 mins
🕐 45 mins

COOK'S TIP

This pizza base is softer in texture than a normal bread dough and is ideal served from the pan. Top with any of your favorite pizza ingredients.

These small potato dumplings are flavored with spinach, cooked in boiling water, and served with a tomato sauce.

Potato *and* Spinach Gnocchi

1 Cook the diced potatoes in a pan of boiling water for 10 minutes or until cooked through. Drain and mash the potatoes.

2 Meanwhile, blanch the spinach in a separate pan of boiling water for about 1–2 minutes. Drain the spinach and shred the leaves.

3 Transfer the mashed potato to a lightly floured cutting board and make a well in the center. Add the egg yolk, olive oil, spinach, and a little of the flour. Quickly mix the ingredients into the potato, adding more flour as you go, until you have a firm dough. Divide the mixture into very small dumplings.

4 Cook the gnocchi, in batches, in a saucepan of boiling salted water for about 5 minutes or until they rise to the surface.

5 Meanwhile, make the sauce. Put the olive oil, shallots, garlic, strained tomatoes, and sugar into a pan and cook over low heat for 10–15 minutes or until the sauce has thickened.

6 Drain the gnocchi, using a draining spoon, and transfer to 4 warmed serving dishes. Spoon over the sauce and garnish with the spinach leaves.

SERVES 4

1²⁄₃ cups diced mealy potatoes
6 oz/175 g fresh spinach
1 egg yolk
1 tsp olive oil
1 cup all-purpose flour, plus extra for dusting
salt and pepper
fresh spinach leaves, to garnish

sauce
1 tbsp olive oil
2 shallots, chopped
1 garlic clove, crushed
1¹⁄₄ cups strained tomatoes
2 tsp soft light brown sugar

COOK'S TIP

Add chopped fresh herbs and cheese to the gnocchi dough instead of the spinach, if you prefer.

NUTRITION
Calories *315*; Sugars *7 g*; Protein *8 g*;
Carbohydrate *56 g*; Fat *8 g*; Saturates *1 g*

⭐⭐⭐   moderate
🕐   20 mins
🕐   30 mins

POTATOES

This is a very colorful and nutritious dish, packed full of crunchy vegetables in a tasty white wine sauce.

Potato-Topped Vegetables

SERVES 4

1 carrot, diced
6 oz/175 g cauliflower florets
6 oz/175 g broccoli florets
1 fennel bulb, sliced
2³⁄₄ oz/75 g green beans, halved
2 tbsp butter
¹⁄₄ cup all-purpose flour
²⁄₃ cup vegetable bouillon
²⁄₃ cup dry white wine
²⁄₃ cup milk
6 oz/175 g crimini mushrooms, quartered
2 tbsp chopped fresh sage

topping
generous 5 cups diced mealy potatoes
2 tbsp butter
4 tbsp plain yogurt
generous ²⁄₃ cup freshly grated
   Parmesan cheese
1 tsp fennel seeds
salt and pepper

1 Cook the carrot, cauliflower, broccoli, fennel, and beans in a large pan of boiling water for 10 minutes until just tender. Drain the vegetables thoroughly and set aside.

2 Melt the butter in a pan over low heat. Stir in the flour and cook for about 1 minute. Remove from the heat and stir in the bouillon, wine, and milk. Return to the heat and bring to a boil, stirring until thickened. Stir in the reserved vegetables, mushrooms, and sage.

3 Meanwhile, make the topping. Cook the diced potatoes in a pan of boiling water for 10–15 minutes. Drain and mash with the butter, yogurt, and half the grated Parmesan cheese. Stir in the fennel seeds. Season to taste with salt and pepper.

4 Spoon the vegetable mixture into a 4-cup/1-liter pie dish. Spoon the potato over the top and sprinkle with the remaining cheese. Cook in a preheated oven, 375°F/190°C, for 30–35 minutes or until golden. Serve hot.

NUTRITION

Calories *413*; Sugars *11 g*; Protein *19 g*;
Carbohydrate *41 g*; Fat *18 g*; Saturates *11 g*

✿✿✿   moderate
⏱   20 mins
🕐   1 hr 15 mins

This soufflé is very simple to make, yet it has a delicious flavor and melts in the mouth. Choose three alternative cheeses, if preferred.

Three Cheese Soufflé

1 Grease a 10-cup/2.2-liter soufflé dish and dust with the flour. Set aside.

2 Cook the potatoes in a pan of boiling water until tender. Mash until very smooth and then transfer to a mixing bowl to cool.

3 Beat the egg yolks into the potato and stir in the Swiss cheese, blue cheese, and cheddar cheese, mixing well. Season to taste with salt and pepper.

4 Whisk the egg whites in a clean bowl until standing in peaks, then gently fold them into the potato mixture with a metal spoon until incorporated.

5 Spoon the potato mixture into the prepared soufflé dish.

6 Cook in a preheated oven, 425°F/220°C, for 35–40 minutes until risen and set. Serve the soufflé at once.

SERVES 4

2 tbsp butter, for greasing
2 tsp all-purpose flour, for dusting
2 lb/900 g mealy potatoes
8 eggs, separated
¼ cup grated Swiss cheese
¼ cup crumbled blue cheese
¼ cup grated sharp colby cheese
salt and pepper

NUTRITION
Calories *447*; Sugars *1 g*; Protein *22 g*;
Carbohydrate *41 g*; Fat *23 g*; Saturates *11 g*

⭐⭐ easy

🕐 10 mins

🕐 55 mins

🧑‍🍳 **COOK'S TIP**

Insert a fine skewer into the center of the soufflé; it should come out clean when the soufflé is fully cooked through.

This attractive and nutritious loaf is also delicious. Served with a tomato sauce, it can be eaten hot or cold with salad greens.

Nutty Harvest Loaf

SERVES 4

2 tbsp butter, plus extra for greasing
2²⁄₃ cups diced mealy potatoes
1 onion, chopped
2 garlic cloves, crushed
4¹⁄₂ oz/125 g unsalted peanuts
1¹⁄₃ cups fresh white bread crumbs
1 egg, beaten
2 tbsp chopped fresh cilantro
²⁄₃ cup vegetable bouillon
2³⁄₄ oz/75 g sliced mushrooms
1³⁄₄ oz/50 g sun-dried tomatoes, sliced
salt and pepper
mixed salad greens, to serve

sauce
²⁄₃ cup homemade crème fraîche or
    sour cream
2 tsp tomato paste
2 tsp honey
2 tbsp chopped fresh cilantro

NUTRITION

Calories 554; Sugars 12 g; Protein 16 g;
Carbohydrate 43 g; Fat 37 g; Saturates 16 g

⭐⭐⭐   moderate
🕐   20 mins
🕐   1 hr 20 mins

1 Grease a 1-lb/450-g loaf pan with butter. Cook the potatoes in a pan of boiling water for 10 minutes, until cooked through. Drain well, then mash and set aside.

2 Melt half of the butter in a skillet over low heat. Add the onion and garlic and cook gently for 2–3 minutes until softened. Finely chop the nuts or process them in a food processor for 30 seconds with the bread crumbs.

3 Mix the chopped nuts and bread crumbs into the potatoes with the egg, cilantro, and vegetable bouillon. Stir in the onion and garlic and mix well.

4 Melt the remaining butter in the skillet over low heat. Add the sliced mushrooms and cook for 2–3 minutes.

5 Press half of the potato mixture into the base of the prepared loaf pan. Spoon the mushrooms on top and sprinkle with the sun-dried tomatoes. Spoon the remaining potato mixture on top and smooth the surface. Cover with foil and bake in a preheated oven, 350°F/190°C, for 1 hour or until firm.

6 Meanwhile, mix the sauce ingredients together. Cut the nutty harvest loaf into slices and serve with the sauce.

🍳 COOK'S TIP

If you prefer, use unsalted cashew nuts instead of the peanuts.

This is a savory version of a cheesecake with a layer of fried potatoes as a delicious base. Use frozen mixed vegetables for the topping, if you like.

Vegetable Cake

1 Brush an 8-inch/20-cm springform cake pan with vegetable oil.

2 To make the base, heat the oil in a skillet over medium heat. Add the potato slices and cook until softened and browned. Drain on paper towels and place in the bottom of the pan.

3 To make the topping, heat the vegetable oil in a separate skillet over low heat. Add the leek and fry, stirring frequently, for 3–4 minutes until softened.

4 Add the zucchini, bell peppers, carrot, and parsley to the skillet and cook over low heat for 5–7 minutes or until the vegetables have softened.

5 Meanwhile, beat the cheeses and eggs together in a large bowl. Stir in the vegetables and season to taste with salt and pepper. Spoon the mixture evenly over the potato base.

6 Cook in a preheated oven, 375°F/190°C, for 20–25 minutes until the cake is set.

7 Remove the vegetable cake from the pan and transfer to a warmed serving plate. Garnish with shredded leek and serve with salad greens.

SERVES 4

base
2 tbsp vegetable oil, plus extra for brushing
2lb 12 oz/1.25 kg large waxy potatoes, sliced thinly

topping
1 tbsp vegetable oil
1 leek, chopped
1 zucchini, grated
1 red bell pepper, seeded and diced
1 green bell pepper, seeded and diced
1 carrot, grated
2 tsp chopped fresh parsley
1 cup full-fat soft cheese
¼ cup grated sharp cheese
2 eggs, beaten
salt and pepper
shredded cooked leek, to garnish
salad greens, to serve

NUTRITION
Calories *502*; Sugars *8 g*; Protein *16 g*; Carbohydrate *41 g*; Fat *31 g*; Saturates *14 g*

easy

20 mins

45 mins

This is an easy, but very filling meal. The potatoes are baked until fluffy, then mixed with a tasty pesto filling and baked again.

Twice-Baked Pesto Potatoes

SERVES 4

4 baking potatoes
²/₃ cup heavy cream
¹/₃ cup vegetable bouillon
1 tbsp lemon juice
2 garlic cloves, crushed
3 tbsp chopped fresh basil
2 tbsp pine nuts
scant ½ cup freshly grated Parmesan cheese
salt and pepper

1 Scrub the potatoes well and prick the skins with a fork. Rub a little salt into the skins and place on a cookie sheet.

2 Cook in a preheated oven, 375°F/190°C, for 1 hour or until the potatoes are cooked through and the skins are crisp.

3 Remove the potatoes from the oven and cut them in half lengthwise. Using a spoon, scoop the potato flesh into a mixing bowl, leaving a thin shell of potato inside the skins. Mash the potato flesh with a fork.

4 Meanwhile, mix the cream and vegetable bouillon in a pan and let simmer over low heat for about 8–10 minutes or until reduced by half.

5 Stir in the lemon juice, garlic, and chopped basil, and season to taste with salt and pepper. Stir the mixture into the mashed potato flesh, together with the pine nuts.

6 Spoon the mixture back into the potato shells and sprinkle the Parmesan cheese on top. Return the potatoes to the oven for 10 minutes or until the cheese has browned. Serve.

NUTRITION
Calories *444*; Sugars *3 g*; Protein *10 g*;
Carbohydrate *40 g*; Fat *28 g*; Saturates *13 g*

easy
10 mins
1 hr 20 mins

COOK'S TIP

Add full-fat soft cheese or thinly sliced mushrooms to the mashed potato flesh at step 5, if you prefer.

This tasty meal is made with sliced potatoes, bean curd, and vegetables cooked in the pan from which it is served.

Pan Potato Cake

1 Cook the sliced potatoes in a large pan of boiling water for 10 minutes. Drain.

2 Meanwhile, cook the carrot and broccoli florets in a separate pan of boiling water for 5 minutes. Drain with a draining spoon.

3 Heat the butter and vegetable oil in a 9-inch/23-cm skillet over low heat. Add the onion and garlic and cook for 2–3 minutes. Add half of the potato slices to the skillet, covering the bottom of the skillet.

4 Cover the potato slices with the carrot, broccoli, and the bean curd. Sprinkle with half of the sage and cover with the remaining potato slices. Sprinkle the grated cheese over the top.

5 Cook over medium heat for 8–10 minutes. Place the pan under a preheated medium broiler for 2–3 minutes or until the cheese melts.

6 Garnish with the remaining sage and serve at once.

SERVES 4

1 lb 8 oz/675 g waxy potatoes, unpeeled and sliced
1 carrot, diced
8 oz/225 g small broccoli florets
5 tbsp butter
2 tbsp vegetable oil
1 red onion, cut into fourths
2 garlic cloves, crushed
6 oz/175 g bean curd, drained and diced
2 tbsp chopped fresh sage
¾ cup grated sharp cheese

NUTRITION
Calories 452; Sugars 6 g; Protein 17 g; Carbohydrate 35 g; Fat 28 g; Saturates 13 g

⊛⊛ easy
🕐 15 mins
🕐 20 mins

 COOK'S TIP

Make sure the mixture fills the width of your skillet so the layers remain intact.

This is a quick dish to prepare and it can be left to cook in the oven without needing any more attention.

Cheese *and* Potato Layer Bake

SERVES 4

2 lb/900 g unpeeled waxy potatoes, cut into wedges
2 tbsp butter
1 red onion, halved and sliced
2 garlic cloves, crushed
¼ cup all-purpose flour
2½ cups milk
14 oz/400 g canned artichoke hearts in brine, drained and halved
5½ oz/150 g frozen mixed vegetables, thawed
1¼ cups grated Swiss cheese
1¼ cups grated sharp cheese
½ cup crumbled Gorgonzola cheese
⅓ cup freshly grated Parmesan cheese
8 oz/225 g bean curd, drained and sliced
2 tbsp chopped fresh thyme
salt and pepper
fresh thyme sprigs, to garnish

1 Parboil the potato wedges in a pan of boiling water for 10 minutes. Drain thoroughly and set aside.

2 Meanwhile, melt the butter in a pan. Add the sliced onion and garlic and cook over low heat, stirring frequently, for 2–3 minutes.

3 Stir the flour into the pan and cook for 1 minute. Gradually add the milk and bring to a boil, stirring constantly.

4 Reduce the heat and add the artichoke hearts, mixed vegetables, half of each of the 4 cheeses, and the bean curd to the pan, mixing well. Stir in the chopped thyme and season to taste with salt and pepper.

5 Arrange a layer of the potato wedges in the base of a shallow ovenproof dish. Spoon the vegetable mixture over the top and cover with the remaining potato wedges. Sprinkle the rest of the 4 cheeses over the top.

6 Cook in a preheated oven, 400°F/200°C, for 30 minutes or until the potatoes are cooked and the top is golden-brown. Garnish the bake with a few sprigs of fresh thyme and serve.

NUTRITION
Calories *766*; Sugars *14 g*; Protein *44 g*; Carbohydrate *60 g*; Fat *40 g*; Saturates *23 g*

easy

25 mins

45 mins

Similar to a simple moussaka, this recipe is made up of layers of eggplant, tomato, and potato baked with a yogurt topping.

Potato *and* Eggplant Gratin

1 Cook the sliced potatoes in a pan of boiling water for 10 minutes until tender, but not breaking up. Drain and then set aside.

2 Heat the vegetable oil in a skillet over low heat. Add the onion and garlic and cook, stirring occasionally, for 2–3 minutes.

3 Add the bean curd, tomato paste, and flour, and cook for 1 minute. Gradually stir in the bouillon and bring to a boil, stirring. Reduce the heat and let simmer for 10 minutes.

4 Arrange a layer of the potato slices in the base of a deep ovenproof dish. Spoon the bean curd mixture evenly on top. Layer the sliced tomatoes, then the eggplant, and finally the remaining potato slices, on top of the bean curd mixture, making sure that it is completely covered. Sprinkle with thyme.

5 Mix the yogurt and beaten eggs together in a bowl and season to taste with salt and pepper. Spoon the yogurt topping over the sliced potatoes to cover.

6 Bake in a preheated oven, 375°F/190°C, for about 35–45 minutes or until the topping is browned. Serve.

SERVES 4

1 lb 2 oz/500 g waxy potatoes, sliced
1 tbsp vegetable oil
1 onion, chopped
2 garlic cloves, crushed
1 lb 2 oz/500 g bean curd, drained and diced
2 tbsp tomato paste
½ cup all-purpose flour
1¼ cups vegetable bouillon
2 large tomatoes, sliced
1 eggplant, sliced
2 tbsp chopped fresh thyme
scant 2 cups plain yogurt
2 eggs, beaten
salt and pepper

COOK'S TIP

You can use marinated or smoked bean curd for extra flavor, if you wish.

NUTRITION
Calories *409*; Sugars *17 g*; Protein *28 g*;
Carbohydrate *45 g*; Fat *14 g*; Saturates *3 g*

moderate

25 mins

1 hr 15 mins

This delicious baked terrine has a base of mashed potato, which is flavored with nuts, cheese, herbs, and spices.

Spicy Potato *and* Nut Terrine

SERVES 4

2 tbsp butter, plus extra for greasing
1⅓ cups diced mealy potatoes
8 oz/225 g pecans
8 oz/225 g unsalted cashews
1 onion, chopped finely
2 garlic cloves, crushed
4½ oz/125 g diced open-cup mushrooms
2 tbsp chopped mixed herbs
1 tsp paprika
1 tsp ground cumin
1 tsp ground coriander
4 eggs, beaten
½ cup full-fat soft cheese
⅔ cup freshly grated Parmesan cheese
salt and pepper

sauce

3 large tomatoes, peeled, seeded, and chopped
2 tbsp tomato paste
5 tbsp red wine
1 tbsp red wine vinegar
pinch of superfine sugar

NUTRITION
Calories *1100*; Sugars *13 g*; Protein *34 g*; Carbohydrate *31 g*; Fat *93 g*; Saturates *22 g*

✪✪✪ moderate

15 mins

1 hr 20 mins

1 Grease a 2-lb/1-kg loaf pan with butter and line with baking parchment.

2 Cook the potatoes in a large pan of lightly salted boiling water for 10 minutes or until cooked through. Drain and mash thoroughly.

3 Finely chop the pecans and cashews or process in a food processor. Mix the nuts with the onion, garlic, and mushrooms. Melt the butter in a skillet over low heat. Add the nut mixture and cook for 5–7 minutes. Add the herbs and spices. Stir in the eggs, cheeses, and potatoes, and season to taste with salt and pepper.

4 Spoon the mixture into the prepared loaf pan, pressing down firmly. Cook in a preheated oven, 375°F/190°C, for 1 hour or until set.

5 To make the sauce, mix the tomatoes, tomato paste, wine, wine vinegar, and sugar in a pan and bring to a boil, stirring. Cook for 10 minutes or until the tomatoes have reduced. Press the sauce through a strainer or process in a food processor for 30 seconds. Turn the terrine out of the pan onto a serving plate and cut into slices. Serve with the tomato sauce.

A mixture of red lentils, bean curd, and vegetables is cooked beneath a crunchy potato topping for a really hearty meal.

Potato-Topped Lentil Bake

1 To make the topping, cook the potatoes in a large pan of boiling water for 10 minutes or until cooked through. Drain well. Add the butter and milk and mash thoroughly. Stir in the pecans and chopped thyme and set aside.

2 Cook the lentils in boiling water for 20–30 minutes or until tender. Drain thoroughly and set aside.

3 Melt the butter in a skillet over medium heat. Add the leek, garlic, celery, and broccoli and cook, stirring frequently, for 5 minutes until softened. Add the bean curd cubes. Stir in the lentils, together with the tomato paste. Season to taste with salt and pepper, then turn the mixture into the bottom of a shallow ovenproof dish.

4 Spoon the mashed potato evenly on top of the lentil mixture.

5 Cook in a preheated oven, 400°F/200°C, for about 30–35 minutes or until the topping is golden. Garnish with sprigs of fresh thyme and serve hot.

SERVES **4**

TOPPING
4 cups diced mealy potatoes
2 tbsp butter
1 tbsp milk
½ cup chopped pecans
2 tbsp chopped fresh thyme
fresh thyme sprigs, to garnish

filling
1 cup red lentils
5 tbsp butter
1 leek, sliced
2 garlic cloves, crushed
1 celery stalk, chopped
4½ oz/125 g broccoli florets
6 oz/175 g smoked bean curd, drained and cubed
2 tsp tomato paste
salt and pepper

NUTRITION
Calories *627*; Sugars *7 g*; Protein *26 g*; Carbohydrate *66 g*; Fat *30 g*; Saturates *13 g*

✪✪✪ moderate
🕐 10 mins
🕐 1 hr 30 mins

🧑‍🍳 COOK'S TIP
You can use almost any combination of your favorite vegetables in this dish.

These strudels look really impressive and are perfect if friends are expected, or for a more formal dinner party dish.

Vegetable Strudels

SERVES 4

filling
2 tbsp vegetable oil
2 tbsp butter
¾ cup finely diced potatoes
1 leek, shredded
2 garlic cloves, crushed
1 tsp garam masala
½ tsp chili powder
½ tsp turmeric
1¾ oz/50 g okra, sliced
3½ oz/100 g sliced white mushrooms
2 tomatoes, diced
8 oz/225 g firm bean curd, drained and diced
salt and pepper

filling
12 oz/350 g phyllo pastry
2 tbsp butter, melted
1 tbsp butter, for greasing

NUTRITION
Calories *485*; Sugars *5 g*; Protein *16 g*;
Carbohydrate *47 g*; Fat *27 g*; Saturates *5 g*

✪✪✪   moderate
🕐   25 mins
🕐   30 mins

1 To make the filling, heat the vegetable oil and butter in a skillet over medium heat. Add the potatoes and leek and cook, stirring constantly, for 2–3 minutes. Add the garlic and spices, okra, mushrooms, tomatoes, and bean curd and season to taste with salt and pepper. Cook, stirring, for about 5–7 minutes or until the mixture is tender.

2 Lay the pastry out on a cutting board and brush each individual sheet with melted butter. Place 3 sheets on top of one another. Repeat to make 4 stacks.

3 Spoon a quarter of the filling along the center of each stack and brush the edges with melted butter. Fold the short edges in and roll up lengthwise to form a cigar shape. Brush the outside with melted butter. Place the strudels on a greased cookie sheet.

4 Cook in a preheated oven, 375°F/190°C, for 20 minutes or until golden-brown and crisp. Transfer to a warmed serving dish and serve at once.

In this recipe, a variety of vegetables are cooked under a layer of potatoes, topped with cheese and cooked until golden-brown.

Vegetable Hotpot

1 Cook the potato slices in a pan of boiling water for 10 minutes. Drain thoroughly and set aside.

2 Heat the vegetable oil in a large flameproof casserole over medium heat. Add the onion, leek, and garlic, and sauté, stirring occasionally, for about 2–3 minutes. Add the remaining vegetables and cook, stirring constantly, for another 3–4 minutes.

3 Stir in the flour and cook for 1 minute. Gradually add the bouillon and hard cider and bring to a boil. Add the apple, sage, and cayenne pepper and season well with salt and pepper. Remove from the heat and transfer the vegetables to an ovenproof dish.

4 Arrange the potato slices on top of the vegetable mixture to cover.

5 Sprinkle the cheese on top of the potato slices and cook in a preheated oven, 375°F/190°C, for 30–35 minutes or until the potato is golden-brown and beginning to go crisp around the edges. Serve at once.

SERVES 4

1 lb 5 oz/600 g potatoes, sliced thinly
2 tbsp vegetable oil
1 red onion, halved and sliced
1 leek, sliced
2 garlic cloves, crushed
1 carrot, cut into chunks
3½ oz/100 g broccoli florets
3½ oz/100 g cauliflower florets
2 small turnips, cut into fourths
¼ cup all-purpose flour
3 cups vegetable bouillon
⅔ cup dry hard cider
1 eating apple, cored and sliced
2 tbsp chopped fresh sage
pinch of cayenne pepper
½ cup grated Colby cheese
salt and pepper

NUTRITION
Calories *279*; Sugars *12 g*; Protein *10 g*; Carbohydrate *34 g*; Fat *11 g*; Saturates *4 g*

⭐⭐ easy
🕐 25 mins
🕐 1 hr

 COOK'S TIP

Vary the vegetables according to taste and availability. Swiss cheese can replace the colby, if preferred.

Fish Dishes

There is no denying that fish and potatoes are a wonderful combination. In these recipes, potatoes are used in a variety of different ways to enhance the fish. They are used to form a crispy coating for cod, and mashed to make the basis of fish cakes and fritters. They are sliced to form part of a layered pie, and sautéed with shallots to create the perfect accompaniment to red mullet wrapped in prosciutto. These recipes also include some interesting flavors from France, such as Cotriade, a satisfying stew of fish and vegetables flavored with herbs. For health-conscious cooks, the nutritious value of these dishes is unbeatable.

This simple dish has a spicy bread crumb topping over layers of cod and potatoes. It is cooked in the oven until golden.

Potato-Topped Cod

SERVES 4

5 tbsp butter
4 waxy potatoes, sliced
1 large onion, chopped finely
1 tsp whole-grain mustard
1 tsp garam masala
pinch of chili powder
1 tbsp chopped fresh dill
1¼ cups fresh bread crumbs
1 lb 9 oz/700 g cod fillets
½ cup grated Swiss cheese
salt and pepper
fresh dill sprigs, to garnish

1 Melt half of the butter in a skillet over low heat. Add the potatoes and cook for 5 minutes, turning until they are browned all over. Remove the potatoes from the pan with a draining spoon.

2 Add the remaining butter to the skillet and stir in the onion, mustard, garam masala, chili powder, chopped dill, and bread crumbs. Cook for 1–2 minutes, stirring and mixing well.

3 Layer half of the potatoes in the base of an ovenproof dish and place the cod fillets on top. Cover the cod fillets with the rest of the potato slices. Season to taste with salt and pepper.

4 Spoon the spicy mixture from the skillet over the potato and sprinkle with the grated cheese.

5 Cook in a preheated oven, 400°F/200°C, for 20–25 minutes or until the topping is golden and crisp and the fish is cooked through. Garnish with fresh dill sprigs and serve at once.

NUTRITION
Calories *118*; Sugars *1 g*; Protein *10 g*;
Carbohydrate *10 g*; Fat *4.4 g*; Saturates *2.6 g*

moderate

5–10 mins

35 mins

🍽 **COOK'S TIP**

This dish is ideal served with baked vegetables which can be cooked in the oven at the same time.

The base for this quiche is made from mashed potato instead of pastry, giving a softer textured shell for the tasty tuna filling.

Tuna *and* Cheese Quiche

1 Cook the potatoes in a pan of boiling water for 10 minutes or until tender. Drain and mash. Add the butter and flour and mix to form a dough.

2 Knead the potato dough on a floured counter and press the mixture into a 8-in/20-cm flan pan. Prick the base with a fork. Line with baking parchment and baking beans and bake the potato base blind in a preheated oven, 400°F/200°C, for 20 minutes.

3 Heat the vegetable oil in a skillet over low heat. Add the shallot, garlic, and bell pepper and cook gently for 5 minutes. Drain well and spoon the mixture into the flan shell. Flake the tuna and arrange it over the top with the corn.

4 Mix the milk, eggs, and chopped dill together in a bowl, and season to taste with salt and pepper.

5 Pour the egg and dill mixture into the tart shell and sprinkle the grated cheese evenly over the top.

6 Bake in the oven for 20 minutes or until the filling has set. Garnish the flan with fresh dill and lemon wedges and serve.

SERVES 4

shell
2²⁄₃ cups diced mealy potatoes
2 tbsp butter
6 tbsp all-purpose flour, plus extra
  for dusting

filling
1 tbsp vegetable oil
1 shallot, chopped
1 garlic clove, crushed
1 red bell pepper, diced
6 oz/175 g canned tuna in brine, drained
1³⁄₄ oz/50 g canned corn, drained
²⁄₃ cup skim milk
3 eggs, beaten
1 tbsp chopped fresh dill
½ cup grated sharp lowfat cheese
salt and pepper

to garnish
fresh dill sprigs
lemon wedges

NUTRITION
Calories *383*; Sugars *5 g*; Protein *25 g*;
Carbohydrate *40 g*; Fat *15 g*; Saturates *6 g*

✪✪✪✪ challenging
       20 mins
       1 hr

This flavorsome and colorful fish pie is perfect for a light supper. The addition of smoked salmon gives it a touch of luxury.

Fish *and* Potato Pie

SERVES 4

2 lb/900 g smoked haddock or cod fillets
scant 2½ cups skim milk
2 bay leaves
4 oz/115 g white mushrooms, cut into fourths
4 oz/115 g frozen peas
4 oz/115 g frozen corn
1 lb 8 oz/675 g potatoes, diced
5 tbsp lowfat plain yogurt
4 tbsp chopped fresh parsley
2 oz/55 g smoked salmon, sliced into thin strips
3 tbsp cornstarch
1 oz/25 g smoked cheese, grated
salt and pepper

NUTRITION
Calories 523; Sugars 15 g; Protein 58 g;
Carbohydrate 63 g; Fat 6 g; Saturates 2 g

easy

15 mins

1 hr

1 Place the fish in a pan and add the milk and bay leaves. Bring to a boil, cover, and let simmer for 5 minutes.

2 Add the mushrooms, peas, and corn, bring back to a simmer, cover, and cook for 5–7 minutes. Let cool.

3 Cook the potatoes in a pan of boiling water for 8 minutes. Drain well and mash. Stir in the yogurt, parsley, and seasoning. Set aside.

4 Using a draining spoon, remove the fish from the pan. Carefully flake the cooked fish away from the skin and place in an ovenproof gratin dish. Set aside the cooking liquid.

5 Drain the vegetables, reserving the cooking liquid, and gently stir into the fish with the salmon strips.

6 Blend a little cooking liquid into the cornstarch to make a paste. Transfer the rest of the liquid to a pan and add the paste. Heat through, stirring until thickened. Remove and discard the bay leaves and season to taste with salt and pepper. Pour the sauce over the fish and vegetables and mix. Cover the fish with the mashed potato, sprinkle with cheese, and bake in a preheated oven, 400°F/200°C, for 25–30 minutes.

COOK'S TIP

For a milder flavor, use unsmoked fish, and replace the parsley with dill.

These tasty little fried fritters make an excellent snack or main course. Prepare in advance because the salt cod needs to be soaked overnight.

Salt Cod Fritters

1 Break the salt cod into pieces and place in a bowl. Add enough water to cover and let stand for 48 hours, changing the water 4 times.

2 Drain the salt cod, then cook in boiling water for 20–25 minutes until tender. Drain, then remove all the skin and bones. Using a fork, flake the fish into fine pieces that still retain some texture.

3 Meanwhile, boil the potatoes in their skins until tender. Drain, peel, then mash in a large bowl. Set aside.

4 Heat 1 tablespoon of the olive oil in a skillet over low heat. Add the onion and garlic and fry for 5 minutes, stirring until tender but not brown. Remove with a draining spoon and drain on kitchen paper.

5 Stir the salt cod, onion, and garlic into the mashed potatoes. Stir in the parsley or cilantro, and the capers (if using). Season generously with pepper.

6 Stir in the beaten egg. Cover the salt cod mixture with plastic wrap and let chill for 30 minutes, then adjust the seasoning.

7 Heat 2 inches/5 cm of oil in a skillet to 350–375°F/180°–190°C, or until a cube of bread browns in 30 seconds. Drop tablespoonfuls of the salt cod mixture into the hot oil and cook for about 8 minutes or until golden-brown and set. Do not fry more than 6 at a time because the oil will cool too much and the fritters will become soggy. Drain on paper towels. Transfer to a large serving plate, garnish with parsley and serve with aïoli for dipping.

SERVES 4

1 lb/450 g salt cod
12 oz/350 g mealy baking potatoes
1 tbsp olive oil, plus extra for deep-frying
1 onion, chopped very finely
1 garlic clove, crushed
4 tbsp very finely chopped fresh parsley or cilantro
1 tbsp capers in brine, drained and chopped finely (optional)
1 small egg, beaten lightly
salt and pepper
1 tbsp chopped fresh parsley, to garnish
aïoli, to serve

NUTRITION
Calories 300; Sugars 1 g; Protein 16 g; Carbohydrate 11 g; Fat 22 g; Saturates 3 g

✪✪✪   moderate

◔   48 hrs 30 mins

🕐   45 mins

This is a rich French stew flavored with saffron and herbs. Traditionally, the fish and vegetables are served separately from the soup, .

Cotriade

SERVES **6**

large pinch of saffron
2½ cups hot fish bouillon
1 tbsp olive oil
2 tbsp butter
1 onion, sliced
2 garlic cloves, chopped
1 leek, sliced
1 small fennel bulb, sliced finely
1 lb/450 g potatoes, cut into chunks
⅔ cup dry white wine
1 tbsp fresh thyme leaves
2 bay leaves
4 ripe tomatoes, peeled and chopped
2 lb/900 g mixed fish such as haddock,
    hake, mackerel, or red mullet,
    chopped coarsely
2 tbsp chopped fresh parsley
salt and pepper

to garnish
lemon slices
fresh dill sprigs

NUTRITION
Calories *81*; Sugars *1 g*; Protein *7 g*;
Carbohydrate *4 g*; Fat *4 g*; Saturates *1 g*

⭐⭐⭐   moderate
🕐   15 mins
🕐   40 mins

1 Using a mortar and pestle, crush the saffron and add to the fish bouillon. Stir and let infuse for at least 10 minutes.

2 Heat the olive oil and butter together in a large pan over low heat. Add the onion and cook gently for 4–5 minutes until softened. Add the garlic, leek, fennel, and potatoes. Cover and cook for another 10–15 minutes until the vegetables are softened.

3 Add the wine and let simmer rapidly for 3–4 minutes until reduced by half. Add the thyme, bay leaves, and tomatoes and stir well. Add the saffron-infused fish bouillon. Bring to a boil, then cover and let simmer gently for about 15 minutes until the vegetables are tender.

4 Add the fish, then return to a boil and let simmer for another 3–4 minutes until all the fish is tender. Add the parsley and season to taste with salt and pepper. Using a draining spoon, transfer the fish and vegetables to a warmed serving dish. Garnish with lemon slices and a few sprigs of fresh dill and serve.

🍵 **COOK'S TIP**

Once the fish and vegetables have been cooked, you could process the soup and pass it through a strainer to give a smooth fish soup.

Try to get small red mullet for this dish. If you can only get larger fish, serve one to each person. Increase the cooking time accordingly.

Broiled Red Mullet

1 For the sauté potatoes and shallots, heat the olive oil in a large skillet and add the potatoes, garlic cloves, and shallots. Cook gently, stirring regularly, for about 12–15 minutes until golden, crisp, and tender.

2 Meanwhile, divide the lemon slices, halved if necessary, garlic, parsley, thyme, sage, and shallots among the cavities of the fish. Season well with salt and pepper. Wrap a slice of prosciutto around each fish. Secure with a toothpick.

3 Arrange the fish on a broiler pan and cook under a preheated hot broiler for 5–6 minutes on each side until tender.

4 To make the dressing, mix the olive oil, lemon juice, parsley, and chives together. Season to taste with salt and pepper.

5 Divide the potatoes and shallots among 4 serving plates and top each with the fish. Drizzle over the dressing and serve with salad greens.

SERVES 4

1 lemon, sliced thinly
2 garlic cloves, crushed
4 fresh flatleaf parsley sprigs
4 fresh thyme sprigs
8 fresh sage leaves
2 large shallots, sliced
8 small red mullet, cleaned
8 slices prosciutto
salt and pepper
4 tbsp olive oil
generous 5 cups diced potatoes
8 whole garlic cloves, unpeeled
12 small whole shallots
salad greens, to serve

dressing
4 tbsp olive oil
1 tbsp lemon juice
1 tbsp chopped fresh flatleaf parsley
1 tbsp chopped fresh chives

NUTRITION
Calories *111*; Sugars *1 g*; Protein *10 g*;
Carbohydrate *6 g*; Fat *5 g*; Saturates *0.7 g*

✪✪✪   moderate
🕐   10 mins
🕐   20 mins

This colorful, flavorsome dish is served cold, and makes a lovely summer lunch or supper dish.

Poached Rainbow Trout

SERVES 4

3 lb/1.3 kg rainbow trout fillet, cleaned
1 lb 9 oz/700 g new potatoes
3 scallions, chopped finely
1 egg, hard-cooked and chopped

court-bouillon

3½ cups cold water
3½ cups dry white wine
3 tbsp white wine vinegar
2 large carrots, chopped coarsely
1 onion, chopped coarsely
2 celery stalks, chopped coarsely
2 leeks, chopped coarsely
2 garlic cloves, chopped coarsely
2 bay leaves
4 sprigs each of fresh parsley and fresh thyme
6 black peppercorns
1 tsp salt

watercress mayonnaise

1 egg yolk
1 tsp each Dijon mustard and wine vinegar
1¾ oz/50 g watercress leaves, chopped
1 cup light olive oil
salt and pepper

NUTRITION

Calories *99*; Sugars *1 g*; Protein *6 g*;
Carbohydrate *4 g*; Fat *6 g*; Saturates *1 g*

⭐⭐⭐ moderate
🕐 25 mins
🕐 1 hr 5 mins

1 To make the court-bouillon, place all the ingredients in a large pan and bring slowly to a boil. Cover and let simmer gently for about 30 minutes. Strain the liquid through a fine strainer into a clean pan. Bring to a boil again and let simmer rapidly, uncovered, for 15–20 minutes until the court-bouillon is reduced to 2½ cups.

2 Place the trout in a large skillet. Add the court-bouillon and bring slowly to a boil. Remove from the heat and let the fish go cold in the poaching liquid.

3 Meanwhile, make the watercress mayonnaise. Put the egg yolk, mustard, wine vinegar, watercress, and seasoning into a food processor or blender and process for 30 seconds until foaming. Gradually add the olive oil, drop by drop, until the mixture begins to thicken. Continue adding the oil in a slow steady stream until all the oil is incorporated. Add a little hot water if the mixture seems too thick. Season to taste with salt and pepper and set aside.

4 Cook the potatoes in plenty of boiling salted water for 12–15 minutes until soft and tender. Drain and refresh them under cold running water. Let cool.

5 When the potatoes are cold, cut them in half if they are very large, and toss in the watercress mayonnaise, scallions, and hard-cooked egg.

6 Lift the fish from the poaching liquid and drain on paper towels. Carefully pull the skin away from each of the trout and serve with the potato salad.

This is a fish pie for impressing your guests! Try piping the potato topping decoratively over the pie—it looks very elegant when baked.

Luxury Fish Pie

1 To make the filling, melt one third of the butter in a skillet over high heat. Add the shallots and cook for 5 minutes until softened. Add the mushrooms and cook for 2 minutes. Add the wine and let simmer until the liquid has evaporated. Transfer to a 6¼-cup/1.5-liter shallow ovenproof dish.

2 Put the mussels into a large pan with just the water that clings to their shells and cook, covered, over high heat for 3–4 minutes until opened. Discard any that remain closed. Strain, reserving the cooking liquid. Remove the mussels from their shells and add to the mushrooms.

3 Bring the court-bouillon to a boil and add the monkfish. Poach gently for 2 minutes before adding the cod, sole, and shrimp. Poach for another 2 minutes. Remove the fish with a draining spoon and add to the mussels and mushrooms.

4 Melt the remaining butter in a pan and add the flour. Stir until smooth and cook for 2 minutes without coloring. Gradually stir in the hot court-bouillon and mussel cooking liquid until thickened. Add the cream and let simmer gently for 15 minutes, stirring. Season to taste with salt and pepper and pour over the fish.

5 Meanwhile, make the topping. Boil the potatoes in plenty of salted water for 15–20 minutes. Drain and mash with the butter, egg yolks, milk, nutmeg, and seasoning. Pipe over the fish and roughen with a fork.

6 Bake the fish pie in a preheated oven, 400°F/200°C, for 30 minutes until golden. Serve straight from the oven, with a garnish of fresh parsley.

SERVES 4

½ cup butter
3 shallots, chopped finely
4 oz/115 g white mushrooms, halved
2 tbsp dry white wine
2 lb/900 g live mussels, scrubbed
    and debearded
1 quantity court-bouillon (see page 146)
10½ oz/300 g monkfish fillet, cubed
10½ oz/300 g skinless cod fillet, cubed
10½ oz/300 g skinless lemon sole fillet, cubed
4 oz/115 g jumbo shrimp, peeled
2½ tbsp all-purpose flour
3 tbsp heavy cream

potato topping

3 lb 5oz/1.5 kg mealy potatoes, cut into chunks
4 tbsp butter
2 egg yolks
½ cup milk
pinch of freshly grated nutmeg
salt and pepper
fresh parsley sprigs, to garnish

NUTRITION
Calories *863*; Sugars *5 g*; Protein *66 g*;
Carbohydrate *60 g*; Fat *41 g*; Saturates *24 g*

⚝⚝⚝   moderate

   10 mins

   1 hr 10 mins

Poultry *and* Meat

This chapter contains a wide selection of delicious entrées. The potato is the main ingredient in the majority of these recipes, but there are also ideas for adding meat, poultry, and vegetables as the main ingredients, so that there is sure to be something for everyone. The recipes come from all around the world—try Potato Ravioli or Curried Stir-Fried Lamb. There are also hearty dishes including Quick Chicken Bake, and Lamb Hotpot. Whatever the occasion, you are sure to find something here to entice you.

Potato cakes are usually served plain. Here the potatoes are combined with ground chicken and mashed banana for a fruity main course.

Chicken *and* Banana Cakes

SERVES 4

2²⁄₃ cups diced mealy potatoes
8 oz/225 g ground chicken
1 large banana
2 tbsp all-purpose flour, plus extra
　for dusting
1 tsp lemon juice
1 onion, chopped finely
2 tbsp chopped fresh sage
2 tbsp butter
2 tbsp vegetable oil
²⁄₃ cup light cream
²⁄₃ cup chicken bouillon
salt and pepper
fresh sage leaves, to garnish

1 Cook the diced potatoes in a pan of boiling water for 10 minutes until cooked through. Drain and mash until smooth. Stir in the chicken.

2 Mash the banana and add it to the potato with the flour, lemon juice, onion, and half of the chopped sage. Season well with salt and pepper and stir the mixture together.

3 Divide the mixture equally into 8 portions. With lightly floured hands, shape each portion into a round patty.

4 Heat the butter and vegetable oil in a skillet over medium heat. Add the potato cakes and cook for 12–15 minutes or until cooked through, turning once. Remove and keep warm.

5 Stir the cream and bouillon into the skillet with the remaining chopped fresh sage. Cook over low heat for 2–3 minutes.

6 Arrange the potato cakes on a serving plate. Garnish with fresh sage leaves and serve with the cream and sage sauce.

NUTRITION
Calories *439*; Sugars *11 g*; Protein *22 g*;
Carbohydrate *39 g*; Fat *23 g*; Saturates *10 g*

✪✪✪　　moderate
　　　　5–10 mins
　　　　25–30 mins

 COOK'S TIP

Do not boil the sauce once the cream has been added or it will curdle. Cook it gently over very low heat.

This layered chicken pie with a creamy sauce is topped with a crisp oat layer. Use strips of beef or pork for an equally delicious dish, if preferred.

Potato Crisp Pie

1 Cook the potatoes in a pan of boiling water for 10 minutes. Drain the potatoes thoroughly and set aside.

2 Melt the butter in a skillet over medium–low heat. Cut the chicken into strips and cook for 5 minutes, turning. Add the garlic and scallions and cook for another 2 minutes.

3 Stir in the flour and cook for 1 minute. Gradually add the wine and cream. Bring to a boil, stirring, then reduce the heat until the sauce is simmering and cook for 5 minutes.

4 Blanch the broccoli in a pan of boiling water. Drain and refresh in cold water.

5 Place half of the potatoes in the base of a pie dish and top with half of the tomatoes and half of the broccoli.

6 Spoon the chicken sauce on top of the vegetables and repeat the layers in the same order once more.

7 Arrange the Swiss cheese on top and spoon over the yogurt. Sprinkle with the oats and cook in a preheated oven, 400°F/200°C, for 25 minutes until the top is golden-brown. Serve the pie at once.

🍳 COOK'S TIP

Add chopped nuts to the topping for extra crunch, if you prefer.

SERVES 4

1 lb 5 oz/600 g waxy potatoes, sliced
5 tbsp butter
1 skinned chicken breast fillet, about 6 oz/175 g
2 garlic cloves, crushed
4 scallions, sliced
2½ tbsp all-purpose flour
⅔ cup dry white wine
⅔ cup heavy cream
8 oz/225 g broccoli florets
4 large tomatoes, sliced
2¾ oz/75 g Swiss cheese, sliced
1 cup plain yogurt
⅓ cup rolled oats, toasted

NUTRITION
Calories 630; Sugars 12 g; Protein 25 g; Carbohydrate 38 g; Fat 40 g; Saturates 24 g

⭐⭐ easy
🕐 10 mins
🕐 55 mins

This pie has an attractive phyllo pastry shell, which has a ruffled top made with strips of the phyllo pastry brushed with melted butter.

Potato, Leek, *and* Chicken Pie

SERVES 4

225 g/8 oz waxy potatoes, cubed
5 tbsp butter
1 skinned chicken breast fillet, about
   6 oz/175 g, cubed
1 leek, sliced
5½ oz/150 g chestnut mushrooms, sliced
2½ tbsp all-purpose flour
1¼ cups milk
1 tbsp Dijon mustard
2 tbsp chopped fresh sage
8 oz/225 g phyllo pastry, thawed if frozen
3 tbsp butter, melted
salt and pepper

1 Cook the potato cubes in a pan of boiling water for 5 minutes. Drain.

2 Melt the butter in a skillet over medium heat. Add the chicken cubes and cook for 5 minutes or until evenly browned all over.

3 Add the leek and mushrooms and cook for 3 minutes, stirring. Stir in the flour and cook for 1 minute. Gradually add the milk and bring to a boil. Add the mustard, chopped sage, and potato cubes, then let the mixture simmer for 10 minutes.

4 Line a deep pie dish with half of the sheets of phyllo pastry. Spoon the sauce into the dish and cover with one sheet of pastry. Brush the pastry with butter and lay another sheet on top. Brush this sheet with butter.

5 Cut the remaining phyllo pastry into strips and fold them onto the top of the pie to create a ruffled effect. Brush the strips with the melted butter and cook in a preheated oven, 350°F/180°C, for 45 minutes or until golden-brown and crisp. Serve hot.

NUTRITION

Calories *543*; Sugars *7 g*; Protein *21 g*;
Carbohydrate *56 g*; Fat *27 g*; Saturates *16 g*

✪✪✪   moderate

        10 mins

        1 hr 15 mins

🍳 COOK'S TIP

If the top of the pie begins to brown too quickly, cover it with foil halfway through cooking to let the pastry shell cook through without the top burning.

This recipe is a type of shepherd's pie and is just as versatile. Add vegetables and herbs of your choice, depending on what you have to hand.

Quick Chicken Bake

1 Brown the ground chicken, onion, and carrots in a large, nonstick pan for about 5 minutes, stirring frequently.

2 Sprinkle the chicken with the flour and let simmer for another 2 minutes.

3 Gradually blend in the tomato paste and bouillon, then let simmer for 15 minutes. Season to taste with salt and pepper and add the thyme.

4 Transfer the mixture to an ovenproof casserole and let cool.

5 Spoon the mashed potato over the chicken mixture and sprinkle with cheese. Bake in a preheated oven, 400°F/200°C, for 20 minutes or until the cheese is bubbling, then serve, straight from the casserole with freshly cooked peas.

SERVES 4

1 lb 2 oz/500 g ground chicken
1 large onion, chopped finely
2 carrots, chopped finely
2 tbsp all-purpose flour
1 tbsp tomato paste
1¼ cups chicken bouillon
pinch of fresh thyme
generous 3½ cups mashed potatoes, creamed with butter and milk and highly seasoned
¾ cup grated colby cheese
salt and pepper
freshly cooked peas, to serve

NUTRITION
Calories 496; Sugars 10 g; Protein 38 g; Carbohydrate 52 g; Fat 17 g; Saturates 9 g

⭐⭐⭐   moderate
🕐   25 mins
🕐   45 mins

COOK'S TIP

Instead of plain cheese, you could sprinkle a flavored cheese over the top. There are a variety of cheeses blended with onion and chives, and these are ideal for melting as a topping.

There are many regional versions of hotpot, all using fresh, local ingredients available all year, perfect for traditional one-pot cooking.

Country Chicken Hotpot

SERVES 4

4 chicken quarters
3 lb/1.3 kg potatoes, cut into ¼-inch/5-mm slices
2 fresh thyme sprigs
2 fresh rosemary sprigs
2 bay leaves
1 cup diced bacon
1 large onion, chopped finely
2 carrots, sliced
⅔ cup dark beer
2 tbsp melted butter
salt and pepper
freshly cooked seasonal vegetables, to serve (optional)

1 Remove the skin from the chicken quarters, if wished.

2 Arrange a layer of potato slices in the base of a wide casserole. Season to taste with salt and pepper, then add the thyme, rosemary, and bay leaves.

3 Top with the chicken quarters, then sprinkle with the diced bacon, and the onion and carrots. Season well with salt and pepper and arrange the remaining potato slices on top, overlapping slightly.

4 Pour over the beer. Brush the potatoes with the melted butter and cover the casserole with a lid.

5 Bake in a preheated oven, 300°F/150°C, for about 2 hours, uncovering for the last 30 minutes to let the potatoes brown. Serve hot with freshly cooked seasonal vegetables, if wished.

NUTRITION
Calories *499*; Sugars *6 g*; Protein *43 g*;
Carbohydrate *44 g*; Fat *17 g*; Saturates *8 g*

moderate

10 mins

2 hrs

🍳 COOK'S TIP

This dish is also delicious with stewing lamb, cut into chunks. You can add different vegetables depending on what is in season—try leeks and rutabaga for a slightly sweeter flavor.

Turkey is especially good with fruit, because it has a fairly strong flavor. The walnuts counteract the sweetness of the fruit.

Potato *and* Turkey Pie

1 Cook the diced potatoes in a pan of boiling water for 10 minutes until tender. Drain and set aside.

2 Meanwhile, heat the butter and vegetable oil in a pan over medium heat. Add the turkey and cook for 5 minutes, turning until browned.

3 Add the sliced onion and cook for 2–3 minutes. Stir in the flour and cook for 1 minute. Gradually stir in the milk and the cream. Bring to a boil, stirring, then reduce the heat until the mixture is simmering.

4 Stir in the celery, apricots, walnut pieces, parsley, and potatoes. Season well with salt and pepper. Spoon the potato and turkey mixture into the base of a 5-cup/1.1-liter pie dish.

5 Roll out the pie dough on a lightly floured counter until it is 1 inch/2.5 cm larger than the dish. Trim a 1-inch/2.5-cm wide strip from the pie dough and place the strip on the dampened rim of the dish. Brush with water and cover with the pie dough lid, pressing to seal the edges.

6 Brush the top of the pie with beaten egg and cook in a preheated oven, 400°F/200°C, for 25–30 minutes or until the pie is cooked and golden brown. Serve at once.

SERVES 4

1²/₃ cup waxy potatoes, diced
2 tbsp butter
1 tbsp vegetable oil
10¹/₂ oz/300 g lean turkey meat, cubed
1 red onion, halved and sliced
2¹/₂ tbsp all-purpose flour, plus extra for dusting
1¹/₄ cups milk
²/₃ cup heavy cream
2 celery stalks, sliced
2³/₄ oz/75 g dried apricots, chopped
1 oz/25 g walnut pieces
2 tbsp chopped fresh parsley
salt and pepper
8 oz/225 g store-bought pie dough
beaten egg, for brushing

NUTRITION

Calories *790*; Sugars *16 g*; Protein *28 g*; Carbohydrate *60 g*; Fat *50 g*; Saturates *23 g*

✪✪✪✪ challenging

🕐 10 mins

🕐 50 mins

In this recipe, the potatoes are cooked in the goulash. For a change, you may prefer to substitute small, scrubbed new potatoes.

Beef *and* Potato Goulash

SERVES 4

2 tbsp vegetable oil
1 large onion, sliced
2 garlic cloves, crushed
1 lb 10 oz/750 g lean stewing steak
2 tbsp paprika
14 oz/400 g canned chopped tomatoes
2 tbsp tomato paste
1 large red bell pepper, seeded and chopped
6 oz/175 g mushrooms, wiped and sliced
2½ cups beef bouillon
1 lb 2 oz/500 g potatoes, cut into
   large chunks
1 tbsp cornstarch
salt and pepper

to garnish
4 tbsp lowfat plain yogurt
paprika
chopped fresh parsley

1 Heat the vegetable oil in a large pan over medium heat. Add the onion and garlic and cook for 3–4 minutes until softened.

2 Cut the steak into chunks and cook over high heat for about 3 minutes or until browned all over.

3 Add the paprika and stir well. Add the tomatoes, tomato paste, red bell pepper, and mushrooms. Cook the vegetables for 2 minutes, stirring.

4 Pour in the bouillon. Bring to a boil, then reduce the heat. Cover and let simmer for about 1½ hours until the meat is tender.

5 Add the potatoes and cook, covered, for 20–30 minutes until tender.

6 Blend the cornstarch with a little water to make a paste and add to the pan, stirring until blended and thickened. Cook for 1 minute, then season to taste with salt and pepper. Top with the yogurt, then sprinkle over the paprika. Garnish the goulash with chopped fresh parsley and serve.

NUTRITION
Calories *477*; Sugars *11 g*; Protein *47 g*;
Carbohydrate *39 g*; Fat *16 g*; Saturates *5 g*

✪✪✪✪　challenging
　　　　15 mins
　　　　2 hrs 15 mins

In this recipe the "pasta" dough is made with potatoes instead of the traditional flour. The ravioli are filled with a rich bolognese sauce.

Potato Ravioli

1 To make the bolognese sauce, heat the vegetable oil in a pan over medium heat. Add the beef and cook for 3–4 minutes, breaking it up with a spoon. Add the shallot and garlic and cook for 2–3 minutes until the shallot has softened.

2 Stir in the flour and tomato paste and cook for 1 minute. Stir in the beef bouillon, celery, tomatoes, and the chopped fresh basil. Season to taste with salt and pepper.

3 Cook the bolognese sauce over low heat for 20 minutes. Remove from the heat and let cool.

4 To make the ravioli, cook the potatoes in a large pan of boiling water for 10 minutes until cooked.

5 Mash the potatoes in a mixing bowl. Add the egg yolks and oil. Season to taste with salt and pepper, then stir in the flour and mix to form a dough.

6 Divide the dough into 24 pieces and form into flat rounds on a lightly floured counter. Spoon the filling onto one half of each round and fold the dough over to encase the filling, pressing down to seal the edges.

7 Melt the butter in a skillet over medium heat. Add the ravioli and cook for 6–8 minutes, turning once, until golden. Transfer to 4 serving plates, garnish with shredded basil leaves and serve hot.

SERVES 4

filling
1 tbsp vegetable oil
4½ oz/125 g ground beef
1 shallot, diced
1 garlic clove, crushed
1 tbsp all-purpose flour
1 tbsp tomato paste
⅔ cup beef bouillon
1 celery stalk, chopped
2 tomatoes, peeled and diced
2 tsp chopped fresh basil
salt and pepper

ravioli
2⅔ cups diced mealy potatoes
3 small egg yolks
3 tbsp olive oil
1½ cups all-purpose flour, plus extra
    for dusting
5 tbsp butter, for frying
shredded fresh basil leaves, to garnish

NUTRITION
Calories 559; Sugars 4 g; Protein 17 g;
Carbohydrate 60 g; Fat 30 g; Saturates 11 g

✪✪✪   moderate
🖐   5–10 mins
🕐   1 hr 10 mins

This dish is delicious if made with tender veal. However, if veal is unavailable, use pork or turkey escalopes instead.

Veal Italienne

SERVES 4

5 tbsp butter
1 tbsp olive oil
1 lb 8 oz/675 g potatoes, cubed
4 veal escalopes, about 6 oz/175 g each
1 onion, cut into 8 wedges
2 garlic cloves, crushed
2 tbsp all-purpose flour
2 tbsp tomato paste
2/3 cup red wine
1 1/4 cups chicken bouillon
8 ripe tomatoes, peeled, seeded, and diced
1 oz/25 g pitted black olives, halved
2 tbsp chopped fresh basil
salt and pepper
fresh basil leaves, to garnish

1 Heat the butter and olive oil in a large skillet over medium heat. Add the potato cubes and cook for 5–7 minutes, stirring frequently, until they begin to brown.

2 Remove the potatoes from the skillet with a draining spoon and set aside.

3 Place the veal in the skillet and cook for 2–3 minutes on each side until sealed. Remove from the pan and then set aside.

4 Stir the onion and garlic into the skillet and cook for 2–3 minutes.

5 Add the flour and tomato paste and cook for 1 minute, stirring. Gradually blend in the red wine and chicken bouillon, stirring to make a smooth sauce.

6 Return the potatoes and veal to the skillet. Stir in the tomatoes, olives, and chopped basil and season to taste with salt and pepper.

7 Transfer to a casserole dish and cook in a preheated oven, 350°F/180°C, for 1 hour or until the potatoes and veal are cooked through. Garnish with fresh basil leaves and serve.

NUTRITION
Calories 592; Sugars 5 g; Protein 44 g; Carbohydrate 48 g; Fat 23 g; Saturates 9 g

moderate
25 mins
1 hr 20 mins

🍳 COOK'S TIP

For a quicker cooking time and really tender meat, pound the meat with a meat mallet or rolling pin to flatten it slightly before cooking.

This classic recipe using lamb cutlets layered between sliced potatoes, kidneys, onions, and herbs makes a perfect meal on a cold winter's day.

Lamb Hotpot

1 Remove any excess fat from the lamb. Skin and core the kidneys and cut them into slices. Set aside.

2 Arrange an even layer of sliced potatoes in the bottom of a 3½ cup/1.7 liter ovenproof dish.

3 Arrange the lamb shoulder chops on top of the potatoes and cover with the sliced kidneys, onion, and thyme.

4 Pour the lamb bouillon over the lamb chops and season to taste with salt and pepper.

5 Layer the remaining potato slices on top, overlapping to cover the meat and sliced onion completely.

6 Brush the potato slices with the melted butter. Cover the dish and cook in a preheated oven, 350°F/180°C, for 1½ hours.

7 Remove the lid and cook for another 30 minutes until golden-brown on top.

8 Garnish with fresh thyme sprigs and serve hot.

SERVES 4

1 lb 8 oz/675 g lean lamb shoulder chops
2 lamb kidneys
1 lb 8 oz/675 g waxy potatoes, scrubbed and sliced thinly
1 large onion, sliced thinly
2 tbsp chopped fresh thyme
⅔ cup lamb bouillon
2 tbsp butter, melted
salt and pepper
fresh thyme sprigs, to garnish

NUTRITION
Calories *420*; Sugars *2 g*; Protein *41 g*; Carbohydrate *31 g*; Fat *15 g*; Saturates *8 g*

⭐⭐ easy
🕐 15 mins
🕐 2 hrs

🍳 COOK'S TIP

Traditionally, oysters are also included in this tasty hotpot. Add them to the layers along with the kidneys, if wished.

In this variation of a traditional Spanish dish, eggs are cooked on top of a spicy sausage, tomato, and potato mixture.

Spanish Potato Bake

SERVES 4

4 cups diced waxy potatoes
3 tbsp olive oil
1 onion, halved and sliced
2 garlic cloves, crushed
14 oz/400 g canned plum
  tomatoes, chopped
2³/₄ oz/75 g chorizo sausage, sliced
1 green bell pepper, cut into strips
¹/₂ tsp paprika
1 oz/25 g pitted black olives, halved
8 eggs
1 tbsp chopped fresh parsley
salt and pepper
crusty bread, to serve (optional)

1 Cook the diced potatoes in a pan of boiling water for 10 minutes or until softened. Drain and set aside.

2 Heat the olive oil in a large skillet over low heat. Add the sliced onion and garlic and cook gently for 2–3 minutes until the onion softens.

3 Add the chopped canned tomatoes and cook over low heat for 10 minutes until the mixture has reduced slightly.

4 Stir the potatoes into the pan with the chorizo, green bell pepper, paprika, and olives. Cook for 5 minutes, stirring. Transfer to a shallow ovenproof dish.

5 Make 8 small hollows in the top of the mixture and break an egg into each.

6 Cook in a preheated oven, 425°F/220°C, for 5–6 minutes or until the eggs are just cooked. Sprinkle with parsley and serve with crusty bread.

NUTRITION
Calories *443*; Sugars *7 g*; Protein *21 g*;
Carbohydrate *36 g*; Fat *25 g*; Saturates *8 g*

easy

5 mins

35 mins

COOK'S TIP

Add a little spice to this potato bake by incorporating 1 teaspoon of chili powder at Step 4, if wished.

This simple dish is delicious as an entrée. Choose good sausages flavored with herbs, or with flavorings such as mustard, or leek.

Tomato *and* Sausage Pan-Fry

1 Cook the sliced potatoes in a pan of boiling water for 7 minutes. Drain thoroughly and set aside.

2 Meanwhile, heat the vegetable oil in a large skillet over medium heat. Add the sausages and cook for 5 minutes, turning them frequently to ensure they browned evenly.

3 Add the onion pieces to the pan and continue to cook for another 5 minutes, stirring the mixture frequently.

4 Stir in the tomato paste, red wine, and the strained tomatoes and mix together well. Add the tomato wedges, broccoli florets, and chopped basil to the pan and mix carefully.

5 Add the parboiled potato slices to the pan. Cook the mixture for 10 minutes or until the sausages are completely cooked through. Season to taste with salt and pepper.

6 Garnish with fresh shredded basil and serve hot.

SERVES 4

1 lb 5 oz/600 g potatoes, sliced
1 tbsp vegetable oil
8 flavored sausages
1 red onion, cut into 8 pieces
1 tbsp tomato paste
²⁄₃ cup red wine
²⁄₃ cup strained tomatoes
2 large tomatoes, each cut into 8 pieces
6 oz/175 g broccoli florets, blanched
2 tbsp chopped fresh basil
salt and pepper
shredded fresh basil, to garnish

NUTRITION
Calories *458*; Sugars *11 g*; Protein *21 g*;
Carbohydrate *34 g*; Fat *25 g*; Saturates *8 g*

✪✪✪   moderate
🕐   5 mins
🕐   30 mins

🍳 COOK'S TIP

Omit the strained tomatoes from this recipe and use canned plum tomatoes or chopped tomatoes for convenience.

Filled with potatoes, cubes of beef, and leeks, these pasties make a substantial meal. They are also perfect snacks for a summer picnic or barbecue.

Potato, Beef, *and* Leek Pasties

SERVES 4

1 tbsp butter, for greasing
8 oz/225 g diced waxy potatoes
1 small carrot, diced
8 oz/225 g beef steak, cubed
1 leek, sliced
8 oz/225 g store-bought pie dough
all-purpose flour, for dusting
1 tbsp butter
1 egg, beaten, for glazing
salt and pepper
crisp salad greens, to serve (optional)

1 Lightly grease a cookie sheet with butter.

2 Mix the diced potatoes, carrots, beef, and leek in a large bowl. Season well with salt and pepper.

3 Divide the pie dough equally into 4 portions. Roll out each portion into an 8-inch/20-cm round on a lightly floured counter.

4 Spoon the potato mixture onto one half of each round, to within ½ inch/1 cm of the edge. Top the potato mixture with the butter, dividing it equally among the rounds. Brush the pie dough edge with a little of the beaten egg.

5 Fold the pie dough over to encase the filling and crimp the edges together.

6 Transfer the pasties to the prepared cookie sheet and brush them with the beaten egg to glaze.

7 Cook in a preheated oven, 400°F/200°C, for 20 minutes. Reduce the oven temperature to 325°F/160°C, and cook the pasties for another 30 minutes until cooked through.

8 Serve the pasties with crisp salad greens, if wished.

NUTRITION
Calories *419*; Sugars *2 g*; Protein *18 g*; Carbohydrate *38 g*; Fat *23 g*; Saturates *9 g*

challenging
10–15 mins
50 mins

🍳 COOK'S TIP

Use other types of meat, such as pork or chicken, in the pasties and add chunks of apple at Step 2, if preferred.

This is a variation of an old favorite—creamy mashed potato and carrot topping is piled thickly onto a delicious beef pie filling.

Carrot-Topped Beef Pie

1 Dry-fry the beef in a large pan over high heat for 3–4 minutes or until sealed. Add the onion and garlic and cook for another 5 minutes, stirring.

2 Add the flour and cook for 1 minute. Gradually blend in the beef bouillon and tomato paste. Stir in the celery, 1 tablespoon of the parsley, and the Worcestershire sauce. Season to taste with salt and pepper.

3 Bring the mixture to a boil, then reduce the heat and let simmer for about 20–25 minutes. Spoon the beef mixture into a 5-cup/1.1-liter pie dish.

4 Meanwhile, cook the potatoes and carrots in a pan of boiling water for 10 minutes. Drain thoroughly and mash them together.

5 Stir the butter, milk, and the remaining parsley into the potato and carrot mixture, and season to taste with salt and pepper. Spoon the potato on top of the beef mixture to cover it completely. Alternatively, pipe the potato on top of the mixture with a pastry bag.

6 Cook the pie in a preheated oven, 375°F/190°C, for 45 minutes or until cooked through. Garnish with a few sprigs of fresh parsley and serve piping hot.

SERVES 4

1 lb/450 g lean ground beef
1 onion, chopped
1 garlic clove, crushed
1 tbsp all-purpose flour
1¼ cups beef bouillon
2 tbsp tomato paste
1 celery stalk, chopped
3 tbsp chopped fresh parsley
1 tbsp Worcestershire sauce
4 cups mealy diced potatoes
2 large carrots, diced
2 tbsp butter
3 tbsp skim milk
salt and pepper
fresh flatleaf parsley sprigs, to garnish

NUTRITION
Calories 352; Sugars 6 g; Protein 28 g;
Carbohydrate 38 g; Fat 11 g; Saturates 6 g

✪✪✪   moderate
         10 mins
         1 hr 15 mins

This is a delicious supper dish for all of the family. Use good-quality herb sausages for a really tasty pie.

Potato, Sausage, *and* Onion Pie

SERVES 4

1 lb 5 oz/600 g waxy potatoes, unpeeled and sliced
2 tbsp butter
4 thick pork and herb sausages
1 leek, sliced
2 garlic cloves, crushed
2/3 cup vegetable bouillon
2/3 cup hard cider or apple juice
2 tbsp chopped fresh sage
2 tbsp cornstarch
4 tbsp water
3/4 cup grated sharp cheese
salt and pepper

1 Cook the sliced potatoes in a pan of boiling water for 10 minutes. Drain.

2 Meanwhile, melt the butter in a large skillet over medium heat. Add the sausages and cook for 8–10 minutes, turning them frequently so that they brown on all sides. Remove the sausages from the skillet and cut them into thick slices.

3 Add the leek, garlic, and sausage slices to the skillet and cook for about 2–3 minutes, stirring occasionally.

4 Add the vegetable bouillon, hard cider or apple juice, and chopped sage. Season to taste with salt and pepper. Blend the cornstarch with the water. Stir it into the skillet and bring to a boil, stirring until the sauce has thickened. Spoon the mixture into the bottom of a deep pie dish.

5 Layer the potato slices on top of the sausage mixture to cover it completely. Season with salt and pepper and sprinkle the grated cheese over the top.

6 Cook in a preheated oven, 375°F/ 190°C, for 25–30 minutes or until the potatoes are cooked and the cheese is golden-brown. Serve the pie hot.

NUTRITION
Calories 399; Sugars 6 g; Protein 14 g; Carbohydrate 39 g; Fat 22 g; Saturates 11 g

⭐⭐⭐ moderate
🕐 5–10 mins
🕐 40 mins

This pie's sauce is flavored with dolcelatte cheese and walnuts, which are delicious with broccoli. This recipe makes 1 large pie or 4 individual pies.

Potato *and* Broccoli Pie

1 Cook the potato chunks in a pan of boiling water for 5 minutes. Drain.

2 Meanwhile, heat the butter and vegetable oil in a heavy-based pan over medium heat. Add the pork and cook for 5 minutes, turning until browned.

3 Add the onion and cook for another 2 minutes. Stir in the flour and cook for 1 minute, then gradually stir in the vegetable bouillon and milk. Bring to a boil, stirring constantly.

4 Add the cheese, broccoli, potatoes, and walnuts to the pan and let simmer for 5 minutes. Season to taste with salt and pepper, then spoon the mixture into a pie dish.

5 Roll out the pie dough on a lightly floured counter until 1 inch/2.5 cm larger than the dish. Cut a 1-inch/2.5-cm wide strip from the pie dough. Dampen the edge of the dish and place the pie dough strip around it. Brush with milk and put the pie dough lid on top.

6 Seal and crimp the edges and make 2 small slits in the center of the lid. Brush with milk and cook in a preheated oven, 400°F/200°C, for 25 minutes or until the pie dough has risen and is golden. Serve hot.

SERVES 4

1 lb/450 g waxy potatoes, cut into chunks
2 tbsp butter
1 tbsp vegetable oil
6 oz/175 g lean pork, cubed
1 red onion, cut into 8 pieces
2½ tbsp all-purpose flour
⅔ cup vegetable bouillon
⅔ cup milk
2¾ oz/75 g dolcelatte cheese, crumbled
6 oz/75 g broccoli florets
1 oz/25 g walnuts
8 oz/225 g store-bought puff pastry
all-purpose flour, for dusting
milk, for glazing
salt and pepper

NUTRITION
Calories *616*; Sugars *8 g*; Protein *22 g*; Carbohydrate *53 g*; Fat *37 g*; Saturates *10 g*

⭐⭐⭐   moderate
🕐   5–10 mins
🕐   45 mins

🎩 **C O O K ' S   T I P**

Use a hard, sharp cheese instead of the dolcelatte cheese, if you prefer.

This pie contains chunks of pineapple—a classic accompaniment to ham— with potatoes and onion in a mustard sauce.

Potato *and* Ham Pie

S E R V E S 4

8 oz/225 g waxy potatoes, cubed
2 tbsp butter
8 shallots, halved
1¼ cups smoked ham, cubed
2½ tbsp all-purpose flour
1¼ cups milk
2 tbsp whole-grain mustard
1¾ oz/50 g pineapple, cubed

pie dough

2 cups plain all-purpose flour, plus extra
    for dusting
½ tsp dry mustard
pinch of salt
pinch of cayenne pepper
⅔ cup butter
4½ oz/125 g grated sharp cheese
2 egg yolks, plus extra for brushing
4–6 tsp cold water

N U T R I T I O N
Calories *887*; Sugars *10 g*; Protein *31 g*;
Carbohydrate *68 g*; Fat *57 g*; Saturates *34 g*

easy

10 mins

55 mins

1 Cook the potato cubes in a pan of boiling water for 10 minutes. Drain.

2 Meanwhile, melt the butter in a pan over low heat. Add the shallots and cook gently for 3–4 minutes until they begin to color.

3 Add the ham and cook for 2–3 minutes. Stir in the flour and cook for 1 minute. Gradually stir in the milk. Add the mustard and pineapple and bring to a boil, stirring. Season well with salt and pepper. Add the potatoes.

4 Strain the flour for the pie dough into a bowl with the mustard, salt, and cayenne. Add the butter and rub it in until it resembles bread crumbs. Add the cheese and mix to form a dough with the egg yolks and water.

5 Roll out half of the pie dough on a lightly floured counter and use to line a shallow pie dish. Trim the edges.

6 Add the filling to the dish. Brush the edges of the pie dough with water.

7 Roll out the remaining dough to make a lid. Press it on top of the pie, sealing the edges. Decorate the top of the pie with the pie dough trimmings. Brush the pie with egg yolk. Cook in a preheated oven, 375°F/190°C, for 40–45 minutes. Serve hot.

This dish is very filling, and only requires a simple vegetable accompaniment or some bread.

Curried Stir-Fried Lamb

1 Cook the potatoes in a large pan of lightly salted boiling water for 10 minutes. Remove the potatoes from the pan with a draining spoon and drain thoroughly.

2 Meanwhile, place the lamb cubes in a large mixing bowl. Add the curry paste and mix well until the lamb is evenly coated in the paste.

3 Heat the corn oil in a large preheated wok over medium–high heat.

4 Add the onion, eggplant, garlic, and ginger and stir-fry for about 5 minutes.

5 Add the lamb to the wok and cook for another 5 minutes.

6 Add the bouillon and cooked potatoes to the wok. Bring to a boil and let simmer for 30 minutes or until the lamb is tender and cooked through.

7 Transfer the mixture to warmed serving dishes and sprinkle with chopped cilantro. Serve at once.

SERVES 4

2²⁄₃ cups diced potatoes
1 lb/450 g lean lamb, cubed
2 tbsp medium–hot curry paste
3 tbsp corn oil
1 onion, sliced
1 eggplant, diced
2 cloves garlic, crushed
1 tbsp grated fresh root gingerroot
²⁄₃ cup lamb or beef bouillon
salt
2 tbsp chopped fresh cilantro, to garnish

NUTRITION
Calories 375; Sugars 6 g; Protein 26 g; Carbohydrate 27 g; Fat 19 g; Saturates 6 g

 easy

🕐 10 mins

🕐 1 hr

COOK'S TIP

The wok is an ancient Chinese invention, the name coming from the Cantonese word for a "cooking vessel."

Bread *and* Cakes

The potato adds an interesting flavor and texture to loaves and cakes. This section includes a range of unusual recipes, and also shows the qualities of the sweet potato in combination with fruit and spices, such as the Fruity Potato Cake, which is ideal for any special occasion. There is also a tempting braided loaf and some smaller treats, such as the delicately spiced Potato & Nutmeg Cookies.

This bread has a delicious cheese and garlic flavor, and is best eaten straight from the oven, as soon as it is the right temperature.

Cheese *and* Potato Braid

SERVES 8

1 tbsp butter, for greasing
1 cup diced mealy potatoes
2 envelopes active dry yeast
5 cups white bread flour, plus extra
   for dusting
2 cups vegetable bouillon
2 garlic cloves, crushed
2 tbsp chopped rosemary
¼ cup grated Swiss cheese
1 tbsp vegetable oil
1 tbsp salt

1 Lightly grease and flour a cookie sheet. Cook the potatoes in a pan of boiling water for 10 minutes or until softened. Drain and mash.

2 Transfer the mashed potatoes to a large mixing bowl. Stir in the yeast, flour, and bouillon, and mix to form a smooth dough. Add the garlic, rosemary, and three-quarters of the cheese and knead the dough for 5 minutes. Make a hollow in the dough, then pour in the vegetable oil, add the salt, and knead the dough again.

3 Cover the dough and let it rise in a warm place for 1½ hours or until doubled in size.

4 Knead the dough again and divide it equally into 3 portions. Roll each portion into a sausage shape about 14 inches/35 cm long.

5 Press one end of each of the sausage shapes firmly together, then carefully braid the dough, without breaking it, and fold the remaining ends under, sealing them firmly.

6 Place the braid on the prepared cookie sheet, cover and let rise for 30 minutes.

7 Sprinkle the remaining cheese over the top of the braid and cook in a preheated oven, 375°F/190°C, for 40 minutes or until the bottom of the loaf sounds hollow when tapped. Serve warm.

NUTRITION

Calories *387*; Sugars *1 g*; Protein *13 g*;
Carbohydrate *70 g*; Fat *8 g*; Saturates *4 g*

✪✪✪   moderate

⏱   2 hrs 30 mins

🕐   55 mins

This is a great-tasting loaf, colored light orange by the sweet potato. Added sweetness from the honey is offset by the tangy orange rind.

Sweet Potato Bread

1 Lightly grease a 1 lb 8-oz/675-g loaf pan. Cook the sweet potatoes in a pan of boiling water for about 10 minutes or until softened. Drain well and then mash thoroughly until smooth.

2 Meanwhile, mix the water, honey, vegetable oil, and orange juice together in a large mixing bowl.

3 Add the mashed sweet potatoes, semolina, three-quarters of the flour, the yeast, ground cinnamon, and grated orange rind and mix thoroughly to form a dough. Let stand for about 10 minutes.

4 Cut the butter into small pieces and knead it into the dough with the remaining flour. Knead for about 5 minutes until the dough is smooth.

5 Place the dough in the prepared loaf pan. Cover and let rise in a warm place for 1 hour or until the dough has doubled in size.

6 Cook the loaf in a preheated oven, 375°F/190°C, for 45–60 minutes or until the bottom sounds hollow when tapped. Serve warm, cut into slices.

SERVES 8

1 tbsp butter, for greasing
1⅓ cups diced sweet potatoes, peeled
⅔ cup tepid water
2 tbsp honey
2 tbsp vegetable oil
3 tbsp orange juice
generous ⅓ cup semolina
2 cups white bread flour
1 envelope active dry yeast
1 tsp ground cinnamon
grated rind of 1 orange
5 tbsp butter

NUTRITION
Calories 267; Sugars 7 g; Protein 4 g;
Carbohydrate 4 g; Fat 9 g; Saturates 4 g

✪✪✪   moderate
🕐   1 hr 30 mins
🕐   1 hr 10 mins

👨‍🍳 **COOK'S TIP**

The sweet potato bread makes an excellent base for open sandwiches. Top with thinly sliced cheese, tomatoes, and arugula leaves.

These have a slightly different texture from traditional cookies, but they are just as delicious served warm and spread with butter. Serve warm.

Potato *and* Nutmeg Cookies

SERVES 8

1 tbsp butter, for greasing
1⅓ cups diced mealy potatoes
⅓ cup all-purpose flour
1½ tsp baking powder
½ tsp grated nutmeg
⅓ cup golden raisins
1 egg, beaten
3 tbsp heavy cream
2 tsp brown sugar
butter, to serve (optional)

1 Grease a cookie sheet with butter and line with baking parchment. Cook the diced potatoes in a pan of boiling water for 10 minutes or until softened. Drain well and mash the potatoes.

2 Transfer the mashed potatoes to a large mixing bowl and stir in the flour, baking powder, and nutmeg.

3 Stir in the golden raisins, egg, and cream, and beat until smooth.

4 Shape the mixture into 8 rounds, ¾-inch/2-cm thick, and place on the prepared cookie sheet.

5 Cook in a preheated oven, 400°F/200°C, for about 15 minutes or until the biscuits have risen and are golden. Sprinkle the cookies with sugar and serve warm and spread with butter if wished.

NUTRITION
Calories *135*; Sugars *6 g*; Protein *3 g*;
Carbohydrate *23 g*; Fat *4 g*; Saturates *2 g*

easy

5 mins

25 mins

🍳 **COOK'S TIP**

For extra convenience, make a batch of cookies in advance and open-freeze them. Thaw thoroughly and warm in a preheated medium–hot oven when ready to serve.

Sweet potatoes mix beautifully with fruit and brown sugar in this unusual cake. Add a few drops of rum or brandy to the recipe, if you like.

Fruity Potato Cake

1 Lightly grease a 7-inch/18-cm square cake pan with butter.

2 Cook the sweet potatoes in boiling water for 10 minutes or until softened. Drain and mash until smooth.

3 Transfer the mashed sweet potatoes to a mixing bowl while still hot and add the butter and sugar, mixing together thoroughly.

4 Beat in the eggs, milk, lemon juice and rind, caraway seeds, and chopped dried fruit. Add the baking powder and mix well.

5 Pour the mixture into the prepared cake pan.

6 Cook in a preheated oven, 325°F/160°C, for 1–1¼ hours or until cooked.

7 Remove the cake from the pan and transfer to a wire rack to cool. Cut into thick slices to serve with a spoonful of mascarpone cheese, decorated with a few strips of lemon rind.

SERVES **6**

1 tbsp butter, for greasing
4 cups diced sweet potatoes, peeled
1 tbsp butter, melted
4½ oz raw brown sugar
3 eggs
3 tbsp skim milk
1 tbsp lemon juice
grated rind of 1 lemon
1 tsp caraway seeds
4½ oz/125 g dried fruits, such as apple, pear, or mango, chopped
2 tsp baking powder

to serve
mascarpone cheese
few strips of lemon rind

NUTRITION
Calories *275*; Sugars *44 g*; Protein *6 g*; Carbohydrate *55 g*; Fat *5 g*; Saturates *2 g*

⚝⚝   easy
🕐   15 mins
🕐   1 hr 30 mins

COOK'S TIP

This cake is ideal for special occasions. It can be made in advance and frozen until required. Wrap the cake in plastic wrap and freeze. Thaw at room temperature for 24 hours, and warm in a preheated medium–hot oven.

Index

A

appetizers 18–57
apples
arugula and apple salad 52
mixed bean and apple salad 47
sweet potato and apple soup 30

B

baked potatoes 15
bakes
cheese and potato layer 132
potato and mushroom 71
potato-topped lentil 135
quick chicken 153
Spanish potato 160
bananas
chicken and banana cakes 150
sweet potato salad 49
bean curd
potato-topped lentil bake 135
stir-fry 118
vegetable strudels 136
beans
fava bean and mint soup 27
garbanzo bean curry 114
Indian bean soup 45
mixed bean and apple salad 47
potato and bean pâté 64
potato and garbanzo bean soup 21
potatoes with a spicy filling 60
beef
carrot-topped beef pie 163
chunky potato and beef soup 44
meatballs in spicy sauce 82
potato, beef and leek pasties 162
and potato goulash 156
beet salad and dill dressing 48
biscuits 172
boiled potatoes 15
Bombay potatoes 102
bouillabaisse 38
bread 168–173
cheese and potato plait 170
potato-filled Nan 72
sweet potato 171
vegetable-stuffed paratas 115
Breton fish soup with cider 33
broccoli
potato and broccoli pie 165

and potato soup 23
broiled dishes
new potato salad 53
potatoes with lime 91
red mullet 145
bubble and squeak 112
buying potatoes 14

C

cake, fruity potato 173
carrots
carrot-topped beef pie 163
and potato soufflé 99
casseroled potatoes 97
cauliflower
potato and cauliflower fritters 67
celery root and leek soup 26
cheese
broccoli and potato soup 23
crumble-topped mash 98
feta and spinach omelet 69
and onion rösti 66
parmesan potatoes 94
and potato layer bake 132
and potato pie 100
and potato braid 170
and potato slices 90
potatoes Dauphinois 95
potatoes with goat cheese 74
three cheese soufflé 127
tuna and cheese quiche 141
chicken 148–167
and banana cakes 150
country chicken hotpot 154
and herb fritters 81
Indonesian chicken salad 55
potato, leek and chicken pie 152
quick chicken bake 153
spicy chicken salad 56
Tom's chicken soup 40
and vegetable soup 41
chili roast potatoes 93
chunky potato and beef soup 44
cod, potato-topped 140
colcannon 84
cotriade 144
country chicken hotpot 154
crab cakes, Thai 78
creamed potatoes 15

creamy stuffed mushrooms 70
croquettes with ham 83
cullen skink 35
curried stir-fried lamb 167

D

deep-fried potatoes 15

E

eggplant
potato and eggplant gratin 133

F

fava bean and mint soup 27
fennel and tomato soup 34
feta and spinach omelet 69
fish 138–147
bouillabaisse 38
Breton fish soup with cider 33
broiled red mullet 145
cotriade 144
cullen skink 35
luxury fish pie 147
mussel and potato soup 39
poached rainbow trout 146
and potato pie 142
potato-topped cod 140
salt cod fritters 143
salt cod hash 77
shrimp rösti 79
smoked fish and potato pâté 75
smoked haddock soup 32
spicy fish and potato fritters 80
Thai potato crab cakes 78
tuna and cheese quiche 141
tuna fishcakes 76
tuna Niçoise salad 54
fried potatoes with onions 85
fries
spicy potato fries 92
vegetable burgers and fries 63
fritters
chicken and herb 81
with garlic sauce 68
potato and cauliflower 67
spicy fish and potato 80
fruity potato cake 173

G

garbanzo beans
    curry 114
    potato and garbanzo bean soup 21
    potatoes with a spicy filling 60
garlic
    fritters with garlic sauce 68
    roasted garlic and potato soup 28
gingered potatoes 88
gnocchi
    potato and spinach 125
    with tomato sauce 62
goulash 156
grilled potato wedges 107

H

ham
    croquettes 83
    lentil, potato and ham soup 43
    potato and ham pie 166
hash
    pepper and mushroom 110
    salt cod 77
hotpot
    country chicken 154
    lamb 159
    vegetable 137

I

Indian dishes
    bean soup 45
    Bombay potatoes 102
    garbanzo bean curry 114
    pakoras 116
    potato and pea soup 22
    potato and vegetable curry 111
    potato-filled Nan breads 72
    potato salad 50
    spicy Indian potatoes 86
    vegetable samosas 61
    vegetable-stuffed paratas 115
Indonesian chicken salad 55
Italian sausage salad 57

L

lamb
    curried stir-fried 167
    hotpot 159
    meatballs in spicy sauce 82
leeks
    casseroled potatoes 97
    celery root and leek soup 26
    potato, beef and leek pasties 162
    potato, leek and chicken pie 152
    potato and bacon soup 42
    sweet potato and leek patties 122
    vichyssoise 31
    watercress vichyssoise 29
lentils
    potato and ham soup 43
    potato-topped lentil bake 135
light meals 58–107
luxury fish pie 147

M

mashed potato 15
meat dishes 148–167
meatballs in spicy sauce 82
mini vegetable puff pastries 101
mixed bean and apple salad 47
mixed mushroom cakes 65
mushrooms
    creamy stuffed 70
    mixed mushroom cakes 65
    pepper and mushroom hash 110
    potato and mushroom bake 71
    potato and mushroom soup 24
mussel and potato soup 39

N

nests of Chinese salad 51
nutritional values 9, 15
nuts
    nutty harvest loaf 128
    spicy potato and nut terrine 134

O

omelet 69

P

pakoras 116
pan potato cake 131
paratas 115
parmesan potatoes 94
pâté
    potato and bean 64
    smoked fish and potato 75
pepper and mushroom hash 110
pie
    carrot-topped beef 163
    cheese and potato 100
    fish and potato 142
    luxury fish 147
    potato, leek and chicken 152
    potato, sausage and onion 164
    potato and broccoli 165
    potato and ham 166
    potato crisp 151
pistou 36
pizza 124
poached rainbow trout 146
pommes Anna 96
potato 7–13
    baked 15
    and bean pâté 64
    beef and leek pasties 162
    boiled 15
    and broccoli pie 165
    buying 14
    and cauliflower fritters 67
    creamed 15
    crisp pie 151
    Dauphinois 95
    deep-fried 15
    and eggplant gratin 133
    and garbanzo bean soup 21
    with goat cheese 74
    in green sauce 105
    and ham pie 166
    leek and chicken pie 152
    and lemon casserole 117
    Lyonnaise 103
    mashed 15
    and mushroom bake 71
    and mushroom soup 24
    and nutmeg biscuits 172
    nutritional value 9, 15
    and pepperoni pizza 124
    potato-filled Nan breads 72
    potato-topped cod 140
    potato-topped lentil bake 135
    potato-topped vegetables 126
    ravioli 157

in red wine 87

roast 15

sausage and onion pie 164

skins and two fillings 46

with a spicy filling 60

and spinach gnocchi 125

and spinach triangles 73

steamed 15

storing 14

and turkey pie 155

varieties 14

and vegetable curry 111

poultry 148–167

Q

quick chicken bake 153

R

ravioli 157

red mullet 145

roast potatoes 15

chili 93

roasted garlic and potato soup 28

rösti

cheese and onion 66

shrimp 79

S

salads 18–57

arugula and apple 52

beet 48

broiled new potato 53

Indian potato 50

Indonesian chicken 55

Italian sausage 57

mixed bean and apple 47

nests of Chinese salad 51

spicy chicken 56

sweet potato 49

three-way potato 104

tuna Niçoise 54

salt cod

fritters 143

hash 77

sausage

Italian sausage salad 57

potato, sausage and onion pie 164

tomato and sausage pan-fry 161

shrimp rösti 79

side dishes 58–107

smoked fish and potato pâté 75

smoked haddock soup 32

soufflé

carrot and potato 99

three cheese 127

soups 18–57

bouillabaisse 38

Breton fish soup with cider 33

broccoli and potato 23

celery root and leek 26

chicken and vegetable 41

chunky potato and beef 44

cullen skink 35

fava bean and mint 27

fennel and tomato 34

Indian bean 45

Indian potato and pea 22

leek, potato and bacon 42

lentil, potato and ham 43

mussel and potato 39

pistou 36

potato and garbanzo bean 21

potato and mushroom 24

roasted garlic and potato 28

smoked haddock 32

spinach and ginger 37

sweet potato and apple 30

sweet potato and onion 20

Tom's chicken 40

vegetable and corn chowder 25

vichyssoise 31

watercress vichyssoise 29

Spanish potato bake 160

spicy dishes

chicken salad 56

fish and potato fritters 80

Indian potatoes 86

potato and nut terrine 134

potato fries 92

sweet potato slices 106

vegetable cakes 113

spinach

feta and spinach omelet 69

and ginger soup 37

potato and spinach gnocchi 125

potato and spinach triangles 73

steamed potatoes 15

stir-fry dishes

bean curd 118

curried stir-fried lamb 167

Thai potato 89

storing potatoes 14

sweet potato

and apple soup 30

bread 171

cakes 119

and leek patties 122

and onion soup 20

salad 49

spicy sweet potato slices 106

T

Thai dishes

potato crab cakes 78

potato stir fry 89

three cheese soufflé 127

three-way potato salad 104

tomatoes

fennel and tomato soup 34

gnocchi with tomato sauce 62

and sausage pan-fry 161

Tom's chicken soup 40

trout 146

tuna

and cheese quiche 141

fishcakes 76

Niçoise salad 54

turkey

potato and turkey pie 155

twice-baked pesto potatoes 130

V

veal Italienne 158

vegetable dishes 120–137

burgers and fries 63

cake 129

chicken and vegetable soup 41

and corn chowder 25

hotpot 137

mini vegetable puff pastries 101

paratas 115

potato and vegetable curry 111

potato-topped 126

ratatouille 123

samosas 61

spicy vegetable cakes 113

strudels 136

vegetarian and vegan dishes 108–119

vichyssoise 31

watercress 29

W

watercress vichyssoise 29